In the beginning

was the Word

and so shall it be again,

and the Word

is the Law,

and the Law

is Love.

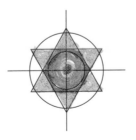

A Leaders of the Way book

DISCOURSES
WITH
MALACHI

Opening to spiritual guidance

by David Davidson

Series Editor: Peter Wheeler.
Copy Editor: Anthea Courtenay.
Continuity: Judith Timmins.
Cover Design: David Davidson.
Cover Illustration: Chris Greene.

Thanks to: Anatole Beams, Ray Poole,
Josef Schmied, Graham Timmins,
and the remarkable and peerless ED.

Special appreciation to Zanne Findlay.

Published by The Leaders Partnership,
a non-profit publishing venture.
PO Box 16457, London, SE14 5WH, UK.
www.arimathea.com
ISBN: 0-9532007-6-0

LP and the star design are trade
marks of the Leaders Partnership.

First edition 2000. Printed in the UK
by Redwood Books, Trowbridge, Wiltshire.
Set in 11 on 14 point Galliard.

To Dad

Discourses with Malachi

The Monograph Series

The Arimathean Foundation has been established to promote and distribute the spiritual teachings of Joseph of Arimathea, Father Abraham and the Prophet Elijah, who currently speak through a deep-trance channel.

Our first publication, *The Way of Love,* is a biography of Joseph of Arimathea told through a mosaic of discussions he had with individuals about the past lives they lived during the time of Christ. Through these verbatim accounts he reveals the story of his family, the events surrounding his life and those of his nephew Yeshua, who was to become the Christ.

The second book, *The Memories of Josephes,* is an intimate account of the life of the elder son of the Arimathean and his relationship with Yeshua. As children they were cousins and playmates; as adults Josephes and Yeshua were companions and confidants. The brilliant images and descriptions that make up this book are memories of a past life, recalled during meditation by the author.

The Way of Truth is an explanation of the simple spiritual truths underlying some of the most perplexing scientific and spiritual riddles facing humanity today.

In addition to these major works, two smaller imprints have been established, the Monographs and the Healing Handbook series. The Healing Handbooks are designed to give those involved in healing and caring for others, simple, practical insights, direct from spirit, to help them, their patients and loved ones achieve optimum health. The first title, *The Way of Crystals,* gives unique and authoritative advice on the use of crystals for healing.

The Monograph series was established so that talks on specific and topical subjects from the three spiritual teachers, as well as inspired writings from the Arimathean Group, could be placed before the public.

The first in the Monograph series was *The Children of Light.* This publication comprises the contents of five hour-long discussions with Father Abraham, the spiritual leader of these children. He has set out the needs, purpose and vision of a generation of very old souls who, with our help and encouragement, will restore balance, harmony and spiritual understanding to a world that is teetering on the edge of disaster.

In the second of the Monographs, *The Way of Soul*, this time based on six talks, Joseph of Arimathea presents a major thesis on soul: what it is, where it comes from, its relationship to God and to humanity, the vital importance of soul in this age and most importantly the pathway of soul, known since the beginning of time as 'The Way'.

In *Discourses with Malachi* a new spiritual teacher is introduced to our publications. During the course of four years Malachi spoke to David Davidson during meditation and the best parts of the dialogue are gathered in this book.

As Malachi prepares his charge for the tasks and opportunities he will have to face in the future, we see the ancient relationship between master and pupil played out. David, living in the world, having to struggle with the immediate trials and tribulations of life, is counterpointed by the thoughtful measure of Malachi. Authoritative, oblique, often dry, occasionally humorous, what makes reading *Discourses with Malachi* rewarding is the universality of the polemic. In David we see the limitations and shortcomings of humanity, in Malachi, the patience and depth of spirit.

Introduction

Malachi is a Hebrew name meaning Messenger. In life Malachi was the great-great-great grandson of Father Abraham of the Old Testament. As a child Malachi knew Abraham, something made possible by the fact that in those days there were only about thirteen or fourteen years between generations. He lived in a difficult time: women were virtually chattels, the religious rules were strict, punishments were harsh and early death due to sickness or famine was commonplace. The strong and the wily survived. Despite all this Malachi developed an under-standing of the difficulties faced by ordinary people; he became a religious leader and spoke out against what he saw as the decay of spiritual values amongst his people. In spirit he is now a Master, a teacher on the Causal plane, which is the last of the seven planes of consciousness, or spheres of light, that surround the earth.

Malachi first appeared in my morning meditations at the end of 1996. I was just finishing writing *The Memories of Josephes,* the biography of a cousin of Christ. Josephes had pre-sented himself in my meditations some three and a half years earlier and I had slowly pieced together the events of his life. I was reluctant to embrace a new teacher and let go of the easy relationship that had developed between us. Josephes was very immediate and personable, and best of all he brought his mem-ories of his beautiful cousin Yeshua. By comparison Malachi seemed dry and dusty, from a barbaric and uncomfortable age. However, he persisted and eventually I began to write down and describe the images that he ignited in my imagination.

As time passed and I collected the paragraphs together, I gradually began to recognise in Malachi a true spiritual teacher. He spoke with depth, gravity and authority, with less of the intensity of feeling that characterised Josephes. Malachi's words were often pregnant with meaning; each time I read them I recognised a new significance or interpretation. He also demon-strated a rather dry wit from time to time; when I was working on the third draft of this manuscript, having completely changed the format with each draft, he commented one morning, 'This book, it is rather like a dog is it not? A hound, a collie, a terrier, each one is completely different but is any one of them less of a dog for it?'

The words in this book are taken from a little over three years of meditations, from 1996 to the beginning of the year 2000, and it is presented in an approximately chronological order. In some ways it could best be described as extracts from a meditative diary, but in this case it has the added benefit of comments and insights from Malachi as well as one or two others. Each morning I sit quietly and if I am lucky I hear his voice, not in my ears but in my heart. Sometimes other aspects of my Higher Self speak but it is by no means guaranteed that someone will step forward. There are many factors that bear on this, the most important being my mood and what I am prepared to accept, but on average I may get a useful paragraph once in every six or eight meditations.

In much of this book Malachi speaks in a didactic way, commenting on my personal problems, or what is occurring on the planet; occasionally he speaks about or to the spiritual group of which I am a member. He also speaks on the demands and promises of the new Millennium. To my mind some of his most interesting comments are about the nature and function of our relationship, how a spiritual being is able to talk to a living man and how this is both served and limited by my attitudes and beliefs. From time to time Malachi communicates with me by involving me in a direct experience of his life. In such instances I literally step into him; I become him, and see and experience what he wants to communicate directly through his eyes, his feelings and the sensations he is experiencing.

How is this book made possible?
Each person has a Higher Self or total soul, an organising principle which is made up of millions of aspects or cells. Ultimately the purpose of the Higher Self is to learn from human life and from free will, and to refine an understanding of certain human qualities such as compassion, wisdom, tolerance and patience. When a child is born, one of the myriad aspects enters into the body of the infant and an individualised soul is born. This aspect can only be born once, but one lifetime is not long enough to learn all the great lessons that life has to offer. At the point of death the soul returns to the Higher Self and the learning that has accrued is shared amongst all the other aspects. Then another aspect steps forward and agrees to take the learning forward another step, carefully choosing the time, place and parents to best facilitate that step. Not all the aspects of a

Higher Self have to incarnate in order to bring fulfilment to the whole; just as a woman may ovulate three to four hundred time in a lifetime but have only one or two children, so the Higher Self may only need a few incarnations to fulfil its purpose. On average, though, it takes about three to four hundred thousand life times to fulfil the learning pattern of a Higher Self.

Malachi has had his life, he can never be born again, but he continues to exist and develop in another realm. Because he is part of my Higher Self, I was born with a residual subconscious memory of his life and times and a connection to his wisdom. Usually someone like Malachi is known as a spirit guide. Like many others who feel that they are guided by spirit in times of stress or difficulty, Malachi is my guide; he has come forward to help me, and through me to speak to others. In my case, practice, some rather reluctant self-discipline and the encouragement of friends has enabled me to recall images from his life and a little of the teaching that he wants to impart.

Who was Malachi?
In his own words: 'I was one within the family of Abraham who achieved a certain prominence, but I was not the only one who did. It was the age of the rule of the father, and the rule of the father was very strict. In my turn I took my place at the head of my family and as the head of an extended family. These families could be quite vast, for it was not just the children that were encompassed but all the servants and their children were accepted and protected as part of the family, too.

'These large extended families were of course the basis, then as now, of tribes. It would be hard today to find a comparison; perhaps certain dynasties amongst the aristocracy would most resemble the kind of relationship and structure but not necessarily the wealth of the family. Towards the end of my life I wrote, hardly as much as you have already written. I taught, I healed through my counsel. I loved the outdoors and the mountains and would spend weeks at a time walking and talking to the people I met. My walks were my meditations, the times when I would hear the voice of my God and it was this ability that gained me such distinction as I achieved.'

I and we
As you read this book you will notice that generally when Malachi speaks he refers to himself as 'we'. This is because he is

speaking on behalf of more than one individual. The Higher Self is collective in nature and when aspects that have lived achieve a certain level of understanding, they are able to entwine their minds with those of all the other aspects within the Higher Self. They are able to draw on the life experience and wisdom of all those other aspects and one can step forward and act as a sort of spokesperson for the entire Higher Self. This is why Malachi most often refers to himself as 'we'. Occasionally when he is speaking strictly of his own life he uses 'I'.

Who is David Davidson?

David and Davidson are actually my father's first and middle names, we share the same christian name. I chose David Davidson as a pen name in honour of my father to whom, although he died relatively young, I always felt very close. At the time of writing I am a forty-nine-year-old man with two adult sons and I have worked as a counsellor, psychotherapist and trainer for the last twenty years. I have been interested in spirituality and philosophy for as long as I can remember. My own particular development began when I was introduced to a remarkable deep-trance medium some fifteen years ago who channelled Joseph of Arimathea. Since then she has also started to channel the Prophet Elijah and Father Abraham of the old Testament.

The channel herself and these venerable spirits have been the guides and teachers who have helped me and many others towards a recognition of our own inner spiritual resources. Perhaps it has been their ability to remain silent at those points when I have been on the brink of some breakthrough or deeper understanding that has been the most difficult and rewarding part of this relationship. At the times when I have demanded the most in terms of explanations and support, they have become their most enigmatic, oblique and mysterious. In response I have become frustrated, angry and blaming; then suddenly I have understood, not by ingesting wisdom from some external source but by understanding it from within. As Malachi puts it, it is as if a door opens on some vast internal treasure house I hardly knew existed. I dare say that in this process they have trusted me far more than I have ever trusted them. Here are some of the little jewels that I have brought out from that treasure house. I hope you enjoy them.

David Davidson, Spring 2000

Malachi now, in his own words

Master Malachi. It sounds rather grand doesn't it? But what does it mean to attain the title of Master in the spirit realms? It is not something that can be achieved in life, but fortunately death is not an end to learning, it really is a new start. So, when I passed to spirit as a very old man and I had rested my fill and made my peace with my life, I recognised the path of learning I had to walk: a vector, a path that I knew would cross with that of another in a way that would enable this channelling at some point in the future, although I did not know when or how. So I walked my path, ever onwards through the spheres of consciousness that surround the earth, understanding many things as I went, meeting other aspects of my Higher Self and learning of their lives. Meeting the great and the small and learning from them all. It is given to some to understand the whole, you see; some are born to act and some are born to make sense of those actions. Usually those who make sense of it all are those who have led a particularly spiritual life and this, apparently, was what I had done.

Achieving mastery means achieving complete knowledge, complete understanding. But that in itself is not enough; mastery in the spiritual sense does not admit those who wish to serve knowledge alone. The blue of knowledge must be blended with the pink of love – which, of course, is why the plane of the masters is purple. So, having achieved knowledge, those who wish to serve as masters must also master love. And who do we turn to for that final finishing school? We turn to the lord of love himself, to Yeshua. It is at his feet that we learn of love. We arrive, thinking we are all-powerful, thinking that there is nothing more for us to learn, and he opens our eyes, he teaches now as he taught then, by example, a love as light as the breath of a mother, as soft as the cheek of a dear one, as gentle as the wing tips of a dove.

It was knowledge without love that brought down the ancients, and it will be knowledge without love that will bring down this civilisation unless love can reassert itself within the hearts of humanity. It is love and love alone that brings meaning to knowledge. It is love that brings the patience, measure and forbearance needed to teach and to learn. It is love that shrinks the swollen head. Many are called to mastery but few are accepted; many step up to that portal only to find that the light that shines from within makes them even more aware of their insufficiencies. Then they have to step back again, to learn, to sit at the feet of the Masters once more.

It is like David here, who writes my words this morning. He would much rather that you heard my words falling directly from his lips, and he tries, he tries every morning, he lifts his tape recorder and steps up to the portal. Sometimes he does manage to speak my words directly. More often nothing comes. Then he hears my words later, a little at a time, as he walks with his dog in the park, as he sits at his computer or as he makes his cup of tea, and he has to collect them bit by bit and laboriously write them down and turn them into paragraphs. It frustrates him, it depresses him, but I understand; I understand because so many times during my own progression I have stepped up to a threshold filled with anticipation and hope and had to turn away defeated.

Then, like him, the pain of my defeat gradually would turn to acceptance, to a recognition of some area that I had not understood properly, and I would find the courage to turn back and apply myself, to learn more thoroughly what I had missed. And in the turning I would find a little more compassion for myself, my expectations of myself would soften and become more realistic, and so my ability to love would improve – a strange way to learn is it not?

Now, in this life, my path has finally crossed with that of David. That which we have prepared for so long can now start in earnest. It is not just two paths that have crossed at this point in history but thousands upon millions. Together he and I can add a small voice to the chorus that will begin; a simple melody at first, perhaps slightly out of tune, but when added to the song of others, who cares? You are only alone to a certain point anyway, and then you realise that you never were.

So here you have a few words of introduction, and I am glad that David is writing them down. I am glad, too, that he would rather speak them. Words that are written can be taken simply as more knowledge, but when they are read aloud or spoken aloud they are subject to the emotion of the reader or speaker. They rise and fall, they shift in tone and cadence, in harshness and softness, they stir the air around them with sympathetic vibrations, they stir the hearts of the listeners. They are clothed in the energy that gave rise to them rather than that which the reader may impart to them. The spoken word is important, especially when the words that are spoken are from spiritual Masters. When such words are spoken out loud they connect directly to the source which gave rise to them, which is spiritual love, which is the Christos. Then those words are like the wing tips of the dove, gently brushing the cheeks of those who are listening, stirring their hearts and awakening them to the truth of their existence.

Peace be with you, Shalom.

Chapter 1

Opening to spirit

My morning meditation, which is essentially when this book was written, involves sitting quietly in my room directly after I have woken up. If I am slightly hypnagogic from sleep it helps. I light a candle and observe the flame for a few moments. I then transfer the golden light of the flame over the top of my head and draw it into my body. I quietly sound three aums and then, if Malachi wants to speak, he will address me. Each of the little sections in this book is the fruit of one meditation. We start with a morning when I was in a hurry and hadn't bothered to light my candle.

Malachi: Where is your candle? It helps so much on these dark winter mornings. [*I light a candle.*] The light that shines within the darkness and penetrates the gloom, is it not? Why would a person, any person, seek to rise above themselves when they are in a difficult situation? No reason at all, except for their inner promptings, inner sentiments, their inner calling. They do it because of the need of the soul to understand, because of the ability of the soul to bring perspective, peace and solace to the difficulties that life presents. Since the beginning of time people have done this, and some of those that have done it have spoken of why it is so important to them to do so. When their words have been written and shared, they have been of so much assistance to others who aspire to spirit. So write our words, my son, and one day they may find their way into the hands of others who seek the truth.

✡

Do you remember? Do you recall? Think back through the years, through the lives until you were me. That same simple core of awareness in a different time, in a different body, a different reality.

David: I can see an image of a man of indeterminate age, older rather that younger, fifties. Long black/grey hair, bearded. He has a staff slightly taller that himself; he is a big man, similar in build to myself but not as tall. Deep set eyes, wild, dark and intense. Robes around his body, not particularly colourful or beautiful, quite worn in fact, and a lot of them considering the heat, gath-

ered at the waist by a leather belt, and on the belt is hanging a pouch. I have the impression of walking, a great deal of walking and a great love of the open air.

This is a description of how you were, of how I was, the same Higher Self, the same wisdom shared by both. Like yourself in this life I would stop and listen to people and then say what I could. It was a very long life and many times I was rejected, turned away, and many times my presence was met with fear; either way my message was not received. Within spirit we have a saying, that it is seldom the speaker who is listened to but those to whom he has spoken. Yeshua did not have either the time or the inclination to write books; he left that to his followers. So often it is the disciple who spreads the word more fully, who can translate the message for the ears of the ordinary man; and yes, I had my followers, many far more skilled and intelligent than myself. But you and I are not to be master and disciple, our relationship is to be more mutual than that. If you will write, I will speak; the more you write, the more I will say.

✡

I have the impression of pale stones and rocks. Mountainous countryside, quite high up. I think that these are the mountains around the area where Malachi lives. I am being shown something of his relationship with this place. He feels a very strong identification with the stones, the rocks, the mountains; he feels them to be living, vibrant things.

When I was young I would spend hours walking alone in the mountains. I felt that in such places I was released from the burdens and expectations of my community and family life. I would walk for hours, for days, with my staff and a little food and water for company. Always there would be someone to stop and talk with. It was not as your life is now in the great city; when I lived, people reached out to one another far more, took far more interest in one another's lives and problems. There was not this privacy that you live with – of course there were far, far fewer people. But when I walked in the mountains it was not just the people I met who were my companions: from a very young age, in the silence and the stillness, I discovered an ability to commune with God. In my mind I would speak to the Creator and a voice would speak back. But it was not only the words that were spoken that impressed me so deeply, it was that this contact brought with it a stillness, an understanding and wonder. I would return from my walks to my family renewed, more willing, more able to take on my share of the chores that life at that time entailed. My family saw this; they recognised what was going on and they made allowances for me and encouraged me.

Because of my talent I gained status, my ability to relate with God was recognised, first by my family and then beyond the family. In some ways I was seen as the successor to the patriarch of our family, Abraham. There were religious rites and observances and it fell to me to officiate at them. I was educated in these ways by the elders. It was nothing like the training of a priest as you know it today; it was rather a training in the calendar of observances, the dates of those observances and how they must be carried out. Today many people who have only a very tenuous or negligible connection with God take it upon themselves to join the priesthood; it has virtually become a form of employment.

In my time, only those who had a very strong connection were invited, although this did not stop those that sought nothing but power. The spiritual connection should precede any life commitment to spiritual observances; it is the connection to source that is of primary importance. You can create your rituals once you have this but it is far more difficult to create the connection from the rituals, although it would appear that this is the understanding in your age. In my day the feast days and observances were extremely rigid. We could not create our own rituals, and those who had the connection were those who were expected to officiate; they were recognised within their own families and beyond. I became known in my own locality and for many miles around. Where I was not known personally my family name would be known and this would be like a passport. I would say, 'I am Malachi from the line of Abraham', and people would say, 'Ah yes! Abraham, that is good, we have heard of Abraham.'

Today, my brother, you have the connection and you are not bound by the conventions of your religion, you stand outside of this. You are free to build all that you wish.

✡

So you wonder, why do I come now and spoil a perfectly good working relationship with Josephes? I come because your progression demands it. Josephes will not go away, any more than your arm or leg can go away; he is your companion for life. But you are beginning to recognise his limitations, just as in time you will become aware of mine. So now you have me as a new inspirer, not in place of, but in addition to Josephes. A new teacher for a new stage of your progression.

But what does this progression serve? Is it so that you can sit back and feel that you have a special relationship with spirit? No, like so many others you have been born to witness and participate in the turning of the age. Christ was born two thousand years ago, at the beginning of the Piscean Age and now we are at the beginning of the Aquarian Age.

Each age is an astrological period, which is also governed by an Archangel whose work it is to give shape and purpose to the energy of God. Uriel, the ruler of the Piscean Age, has presided over the pursuit of knowledge through heroic endeavours. The material sciences are now at a peak, so much so that they have begun to threaten the survival of the planet itself. But Pisces is also an age of duality, when humankind tend to experience themselves as separate from the things they need and desire, be it status, money, wealth or God.

The Aquarian Age, presided over by the Archangel Michael, brings a completely different energy. The Aquarian Age is an age of immanence, an age of wholeness, when humanity will truly begin to accept God within, not as an aging bearded gentleman but as a vital, living, creative force. But it will not just be God the Creator that humanity will accept: God is a trinity. The second aspect is the love principle, known as the Christos, and the third was created when the Christos incarnated as a man, known to his family and friends as Yeshua and later as Jesus the Christ. Never before has this happened and never will it happen again.

This is why the Aquarian Age is also known as the age of the risen Christ: in accepting God humankind will accept the Christ; in accepting Christ they will accept the man; in accepting the Man they will accept the depth of spirituality that resides in their own humanity. And then the world teacher will break free from the yoke of ideology and open like a flower in the hearts of humankind. Humanity has not even begun to understand the gift of Christ; the gift of Christ is the realisation of Christ within, which is the true destiny of every one of you. In different ways everyone is being prepared for this transition, and we have come to prepare you, to prepare you; to explain to you and yes, to encourage you to write these explanations down so that others can read them, discuss them and compare them with their own understanding.

Transitions like this take time, and this one will take tens and hundreds of years. We humbly ask you and others like you, the writers, the artists, the poets, those who work for the good of humanity, those who are open to the voice of spirit, to plant the seeds that will eventually grow into trees that will bear their sweetest fruit long after you have returned to spirit. Plant for your children, for your children's children, for vision.

✡

It is axiomatic to say that all is one and one is all. But these principles, however well understood, do not explain how it is that man and man alone can feel himself to be separate. The animals, the plants, the minerals: none are capable of feeling alienation. In all creation it is man alone who considers himself to be separate. This capacity for alienation and separation mirrors the ability within man to separate himself from his true nature, which is soul.

Man is one in God and God is in all creation. As you look at your candle flame during meditation you see a perfect chemical reaction, contained, complete in itself. The flame does not consume the room, neither does it flicker and go out. Within certain boundaries the candle will burn, it will light, it will illuminate the darkness. It will be true to the circumstances of nature that surround it, it has no choice other than to obey the laws that created it.

Man has the capability to step outside this reality; his nature is vast, he has the capacity to be true to many different aspects of this nature and they are all aspects of soul – even greed, hatred, envy, they are all aspects of soul. So when we say that man has the capacity to separate himself from his nature, what do we mean? If all aspects of his nature are soul, how can he separate himself?

Neither man nor soul is perfect. All is one, but within that oneness there is an energy that is closer to God. That energy, the most powerful energy in the universe, is love. Soul, with its more refined nature, is in closer harmony with this love. It is the work of man to come to know this, learn this and live this with absolute certainty for himself. This task takes many, many life-times, held in continuity by the laws of karma, the laws of cause and effect, and the constancy of soul. The true nature of man is love, the true nature of love is God.

The one is love, the all is the diversity which exists within love. Those aspects of the diversity which are not loved are alienated – not by God, this is impossible, but by man himself. Those people that cannot love do not feel that they belong. All belong to God, all have the capacity to love, and that love can be directed to any aspect of the self or to any other person or thing. Alienation, the sense of not belonging, and all those problems that arise from this state, derive from the feeling that some things are unlovable; but this is not true.

✡

Humanity is like a child which has lost its way, who lives wild amongst the animals without the the loving guidance of a parent. And yet deep within that child the guidance is avail-able; it is present for those who turn inward and take the hand that Christ offers. It is the work of those who understand this to lead the way, to demonstrate through teaching, and espe-cially through example, how to turn within, how to grasp that proffered hand and how to walk in love and understanding. But how to grasp the hand? Do not look to others for a solution to your problems; there are no victims of circumstance, only lessons to be learned. Recognise the existence of the soul; recognise a life beyond the material, a life that is inner, deeper: this is the first step.

Turning within sounds a great deal easier than it is, for few can live with the truth about themselves. Each layer must be looked upon, confronted and set aside; truly it is a heroic journey. It is easy to say, 'Oh, I like myself well enough' in the light of the day when all is right with the world, but what of the self of nightmares, what of the self of fear and dread? It is easy to confront that which pleases us, but to confront that which displeases within the self ... it is easier to ignore it. So, simply to turn within is not as easy as it seems. Whether in prayer or in meditation, the self must be confronted and embraced. Then in time there will be felt a gentle hand. Perhaps at your back during a difficult period, perhaps before you pointing the way, perhaps beside you as a companion along the way. At first you will ignore it, explain it away as imagination; but before long you will recognise it, come to rely on it as a friend in need, and you will realise that it has always been there. There is nobody who does not have it; the only thing that is lost in the travails of life is the sight of it.

We watch the faltering steps of humanity, the eternal repetition of mistakes, as generation after generation walks the same path as their forebears. We do not blame, we do not judge; have we not walked that way ourselves? The world is such a confusing place, where good so often appears to be bad and bad appears as good, and we think constantly, 'How can we help?' To interfere or intervene would negate the privilege of free will; it would negate the unique capacity within humankind for self-determination. We can watch, we can wait, we can advise those who turn to us, but we do not blame those who ignore our love. We understand how insubstantial our ghostly arms can feel when we reach down to embrace you. We understand, my son; but we are not without our feelings, and sometimes our grief at the apparent incapacity of man to receive from spirit is felt very deeply.

We are here for those who turn to us, for those who turn inward, and that turning is a turning in faith. Imagine driving a car: outside it is night, it may be raining and cold; inside you are warm and secure – perhaps you have passengers to accompany you – and the journey is swift, the destination assured. This is like a life without a spiritual dimension. What do you see of the countryside, the nature that surrounds you? You see nothing. Turning to spirit is like stopping that car and resolving to walk the remainder of the journey. The rewards in the short term are not more power but less, not more comfort but less. On the other hand, what the walk can offer is direct experience of the road, a relationship with the things that support and surround you. Such a walk opens the soul to the immanence of God.

✡

Be as ordered in your thinking as possible: this enables an open-mindedness. The ordered mind is not so prey to vagaries of mood and feeling. Once this is established there is the question of inclination, the inclination to believe one thing over another. Suppose we were able to manifest some phenomenon to a large group of people, something slightly outside the norm. The scientists in that group would seek to understand how it happened, how to replicate it and how it could then be applied to other things. The spiritualists might see it as evidence that there is a God, that the spirit world exists and that their beliefs are true. Those with a philosophical bent might ask what it means. The person in the street might dismiss it, fear it or ridicule it.

It would appear that there is an innate inclination in individuals to believe one thing or another and argument, it seems, seldom shifts a person from one camp of belief to another. This is because the inclination is essentially from the soul; it focuses the direction of thought, the interpretation of the senses, in one particular direction or another. There are rationalists, mystics, philosophers, pragmatists, politicians, and all of these various inclinations are serving that particular soul's journey of understanding, that which the soul wishes to learn. When the scientist dismisses the spiritual or the mystic dismisses rationality, it may be that each one is simply trying to understand the same thing but from a different perspective. There is one truth, but that truth can be understood in many different ways.

Imagine a man within a sealed room. Inside he has a lantern; it is lit and it has many different panes of coloured glass through which the light shines. Outside there are people gathered who want to know what he has in there, but he can only communicate by shouting through the wall. So he shouts, 'What I have in here is beautiful, it is made of brass and has a flame inside.' And the people go away thinking they have learned. Then a week later they come back and listen again and the man shouts, 'The walls of this room dance with coloured light.' And those who like colour are elated, while those who believed it was an object made of brass and fire are a little disappointed, and start to question the integrity of man in the room. The third week they gather, and our poor friend in the room yells, 'It is very hot, it smells and it drinks oil.' Now he has lost all credibility. But in fact he has spoken no lie; the fault lies in the inability of those who listen to add the pieces together and imagine that which they have never seen.

The Higher Self, or total soul, is many-faceted, a great glittering jewel of potential. Each time an aspect of the Higher Self incarnates as an individualised soul, learns from life and then returns from whence it came, one of those facets is cut, is polished and can reflect the light. Through that facet the whole can then be glimpsed. But the Higher Self does not want to learn the same lesson over and over again; it seeks diversity of experience and this diversity is reflected in humankind. So you have the totality that is the mind of God, trying to communicate the truth, and this truth is heard in many diverse ways. It is not just the mental perspective that this affects: it is race, gender and creed. So you see, here you have the basis of union and cooperation, and of diversity and separation.

✡

Early this morning I had a dream, and in the dream I recognised that my daily waking life was itself a dream, and that the dreamer was in spirit.

This of course is a poetic way of describing the truth. There is an enormous 'stepping down' of consciousness, of energy, when an aspect of the Higher Self enters a body. In truth the world that you see around you is an agreement of perception or a contract of belief. You say, 'I will sit in this chair and it will support me,' and it does. But there are many others, those in spirit, who would sit in a chair such as the one that you are sitting in now and pass through it. They have a different agreement, a different contract of belief. It is more complex than this in reality, but at the same time the principle that governs this is quite a simple one. The Higher Self is essentially in spirit, it is the author, but it is the actions of the individual that write the words upon the pages of life.

✡

Chapter 2

Meditations and Inspirations

This next section is a collection of insights and commentaries from Malachi on the events of my life. Each one is discrete and stands alone, although I have gathered some together because they are on a similar subject. Mostly they are self-explanatory, they have a universal quality and need little or no introduction. The first came while I was sitting under a tree meditating in the New Forest.

There is such beauty here! The beauty of nature never ceased to enthral me when I walked the earth, but the beauty of the nature that surrounds you is quite different, so verdant. So many look upon it and wonder what they can do with it, how it can be cut, how it can be cultivated, how it can be turned and put to the use of man. But this has nothing really to do with nature; nature is, and is that not enough?

There were times when I was upon the earth when I would stop and pause, just as you are now doing, in a place of beauty. I, too, would sit in contemplation and listen to the inner voice and join my appreciation with the appreciation of those who guided me.

There is no real secret to prophecy; it is no different from what you are doing now, listening to the voices within and then speaking their words. The messages of spirit are simple. When you hear assertions that are wild, complicated, fantastic, it is better to ignore them. Those that have true meaning are those that speak to your heart, that acknowledge and appreciate the very nature of human existence with all its glories and failings. Those voices that admonish, that berate, that punish, that point out your wrongdoings or that deny and defend, are not the true voices of spirit. Those that bring understanding, that are spoken softly, with love and compassion, these are the true voices of spirit.

The more one advances within the spirit spheres, the simpler becomes the message. Those voices which bring admonition, however cleverly concealed, are from those that still retain their earthly ways of thinking, who never really understood their own humanity in life. Just as now you sit in this forest, you feel the warmth of the sun on your back and the gentle breeze in your face, the interplay of sunlight on the trees. The ground supports you and that which you lean against is firm and strong, everything is in place, everything is in balance. Not one element within this scene conflicts with any other. Just as true spirit does not conflict with the human condition, it augments it like the sun coming out from behind a cloud, nothing within the scene truly changes with the shift from shadow to light; it just glows with life and warmth.

The messages of spirit are simple, they bring understanding, they bring peace.

✡

I have been compiling a book of the teachings of Joseph of Arimathea. In some ways I find compiling and editing the words of someone else much harder than writing my own. Anyway, this next entry came when I reached the point of 'maximum chaos' in the editing and was starting to despair that I would ever be able fit it all together again.

In every endeavour there comes a point when you sit with all the elements around you and wonder if you will ever be able to assemble them into a coherent shape. To disassemble and reassemble, this is the creative process; after all, there are no new elements, whatever you build from has always been. The clay that makes bricks, that makes houses, has always existed, it is used in a different way, that is all. So it is with words, the ideas that they express, they too have always existed, but over the course of time some are expressed more elegantly, more beautifully, while others are lost over the horizon.

The spiritual principles that give rise to words are eternal. They sit like beacons, they radiate light. Some perceive that light from a distance, dimly, while others perceive it brilliantly; they are able to describe it from close up. Like the elements, the principles do not change; the vantage point does, the ability to understand does, and the perception of them does. There must be a constant rearticulation of those principles at all levels within humanity so that people can continue to move towards those beacons. It is the destiny of every single person who is born to know those principles, those truths, to embody them and to become them.

✡

While it is a pleasure to talk to Malachi, in some ways it is very difficult to open up to what he says, perhaps because his light casts shadows in me that I don't want to see, his words invite changes in my attitudes and perspectives. At least in the past I had a choice about spiritual guidance; I could pick up a book or put it down whenever I chose. Having an internal source is a different kettle of fish altogether, I often feel I am failing what he offers.

My son, understanding the ways of the ancients, who knew far more than humanity now knows, to have this information passed from generation to generation and down the bloodlines of the chosen is no different from the spiritual transmission that is now taking place. There is truth in what is written in books, yes, and it is good to read it and study it, but there is also the truth of the heart; and attaining the truth of the heart is a harder path. To bring great profit requires great effort, which humankind does not find easy. But we can help with this in your case; we can lend strength to your arm, with a desire that overcomes desire. You have reached towards us and now we reach towards you. Your development has been watched by us, we have seen your struggles, your triumphs, your failings and even your humiliation. But we do not judge; how could we? Have we not walked this path ourselves? Do you not find your feet located in our footsteps?

Those difficulties you encounter, have we not encountered them too? Do you think that you are the first to stray and return, to stray and return? The path is not straight, my son; those who walk a straight path learn nothing from life, so fear not too much for your insufficiencies. What is unfit within you is the very thing that fits you for the tasks that lie ahead. There can be no risk of arrogance or inflation; it is always the most human who are the most blessed. Is it not said that it is the greatest sinners for whom God reserves the best places?

✡

We welcome you to our realm. When you sound your particular note you raise your consciousness to that of the Causal plane. It is not actually higher, it is all around you; it is just like tuning an instrument to a certain note. What then is the Causal plane, the last plane of human consciousness, that which once gone beyond cannot be returned to? It is known to you as the plane of the Masters. In other traditions it has been described as the Devachanic plane, the higher mental plane, or the plane which mediates the energy of God to the human realm. But we prefer simply the Causal plane.

It is not a place, it is not even a plane; it is nothing more than a particular frequency of light, awareness and comprehension that has to do with the soul's command and understanding of the lives that it has led. It is the awareness of being at cause rather than being at the effect. And what does it mean to be at cause? In the words of your Indian friends it means to be impeccable: that is, to be focused on the purpose of the soul, on the purpose and the will of God, rather than the personal or free will, which the will of God embraces.

You spend many, many lives working through difficulties, learning to manage your needs, but when the understanding of the Causal is reached in spirit all this learning is turned, transformed by understanding, and put to the purpose of the soul and humanity. It could be said that those on the Causal have one eye on God and one eye on humanity, whereas those on the other levels of consciousness have one-and-a-half eyes on humanity and only half an eye on God.

The other planes are essentially a continuation of the learning that was undertaken in physical form; for those on these planes there is a certain amount of turning back, of offering assistance to humanity, but this too is part of the learning process. It is only at the level of the Causal that this experience is fully free, fully available for the purposes for which it was originally conceived.

✡

So, it is holiday time, and we find you resting. This is not a time for instruction or to talk about the problems that you face in your development and work; it is a time when your own needs are foremost. It is rare, is it not, to find you in this state? Perhaps once or twice a year, you allow yourself to do nothing. To us it makes you very accessible and in many ways it would elate us if you could always live as you have been living in these past few days, but we know that that is not possible. There is work to do, food to lay on the table and purpose seldom manifests without activity. We present before you a dawn of sorts ...

David: I can see a black landscape with a horizon, not moun-tainous but stark and flat. Above the horizon line there is a wash of colour starting with deep gold and then blending with yellow, primrose and pale blue. Next there are delicate pale greens and jades deepening to emerald, olive and the most incredible dark greens. As I look up I see the greens giving way to turquoise blues and indigos and purples. As I watch I see movement, and coming over the horizon there are yellows and golds fading into umbers and oranges and then reds and pinks and rubies, the most incred-ible crimsons and dark, dark red come over the horizon ... I turn around and look at the horizon behind me and I see that the sky is filled from one horizon to the other on all sides with this vibrant living rainbow ... Under my feet the ground begins to dissolve and I recognise that I am within an entire sphere of rainbow colours.

This is the rainbow sphere in which you are very welcome. Within this sphere are held the teachings of all disciplines, dis-tinct and yet complementary. This sphere and the many others like it do not teach in the way that you understand the kind of teaching you receive from us. When you come here you are really tuning in to a different type of consciousness; you partic-ipate in what is here, you give to it your knowledge and the knowledge that is stored here is transmitted to you, moderated by your Higher Self, so that you receive what you need. What is transmitted is not given in words but in energy, in light. When you come here you must trust this direct transmission, it will be deciphered by you into words and understanding later. All that is necessary for you to do is to be present.

✡

Another new year. Can you imagine an existence without time? It is difficult; you watch things grow; you watch things decay, you watch your own body become older; the weeks pass, the months and the years; the seasons turn. What was once barren is now full of life and growth, what was once empty is now filled with plenty and then that plenty is gone and the soil is bare again. You are surrounded by time and your life is a passage through time. But in our world, the world of spirit, there is no time; nothing decays, nothing grows. There is only the eternal now, and the ceaseless movement of energy and thought within that moment.

So as you mark the passage from one year to the next, rejoice in time, for it is not just at the time of the new year that the old dies and the new is born. This happens at every single moment of your life; you are being born to the new at every single moment that you live, and with every birth, every moment of newness there is another choice: Do I continue in the way that I have been doing? Or do I change direction? Do I stop doing this or do I continue? Time is a most creative medium, for in time you can build whatever you want. Now, at the time of the new year you pause, you reflect on what has been, you reflect on where you are going, and you consider the upcoming year: will it be a repetition of the last, or will it be something new? And if it is to be something new, who will guide me in my choices, how will I change it?

Your hopes can change it, your dreams can change it, your spiritual teachers can show you the way. They can help you use this medium of time to create the Age of Gold. All that stands between yourself and the future is your past, so let go that which no longer has use, take the beautiful light of the future into your heart, and step forward with confidence.

✡

The following was rather a difficult meditation in the sense that it took over half an hour just to speak these few words. It is a shame when I read it through that writing cannot fully capture the feelings that were expressed. The words were spoken slowly and with great gravity.

Consider the following statement: You are what you are, not because you made it so but because you were made in the likeness of God. That is quite a statement, is it not? Now consider this: What is around you belongs not to man but, like you, was created by God and thus belongs to God.

There is nothing in creation that is not of God; every single last little thing is part of God's creation. You are created at one with this force; you are an emanation of the mind of God, of the heart of God. You are the emanations of God, each one of you a cell within the body of God. When we talk of God we talk not of a small God, an old man upon a cloud, but of an energy that contains all things, a presence that is truly vast.

So there is God, there is the Higher Self, there is the soul, there is the self, there is the finite physical body, each within the other, but at this time extended in this order like a telescope. Ultimately this telescope will fold back into itself. Ultimately you will once again be one with the Creator, you will be with God. For all that will remain of you will be that which started the journey and the understanding that was gained upon it.

✡

I have been thinking about how difficult the most simple things are, like getting on with other people or refraining from judging others, and how difficult it is to create harmony.

There is a side to human nature that is never satisfied, that is always comparing, always expecting, always seeking control. When the need of the self is to survive physically, emotionally and mentally, this side of human nature comes to the fore. Whenever it perceives fear or danger it takes over, almost without your bidding. How can there ever be harmony when you ride such a mount as this?

We do not disparage the need to survive. In fact we wish that some would take it more seriously; without your survival there would be no banding together, no work, no message. But your need to survive was never meant to run your lives. It is fortunate, then, that there is another side to your nature and that you have choice. The personality is never satisfied and it cannot create harmony from within itself alone. Once you accept this, harmony is easier to create, for you can then focus your attention on the light of the soul. The soul alone can create harmony within; the soul with its wisdom and understanding, with its connection to the divine is the horseman of the gods. It accepts the need and the power of its mount and neither allows it to run wild nor bridles it too harshly.

So harmony starts from within, from understanding your strengths and limitations. Understanding your role in life and accepting it, this is essential. If each person who aspires to spiritual service could do just this they would find that their acceptance of others would present no problems at all.

✡

Greetings my son, you called for our assistance?

My attention has been so focused on practicalities of late, I want to know that you are still there. Although I meditate every morning my mind is full of all the pressing practical details and plans about the tasks I have to accomplish, and I am sure this affects my receptivity to spirit.

We have been aware of this. It is very hard, even impossible to focus in meditation when the attention is taken up so intently on those things that need doing practically and physically. But it is not this, we feel, that fills your mind; it is a question of responsibility, of looking out for the whole – yourself, your family, your work and your spiritual community with all its interrelated aspects – that consumes you. To focus inwardly and meditate in such circumstances is very difficult ... You could say that we stand back during a period such as this, but this would not entirely be true. When we say we stand back, we stand back from your awareness but we make ourselves felt in other ways, providing energy, providing inspiration, feeding your common sense as you go about your duties.

✡

The morning before a teaching weekend I wait 20 minutes in meditation before contact with Malachi.

Any amount of waiting will not bring what is desired if what is desired does not wish to come. We say this to you this morning that you may understand our reluctance in coming forward. It is not that we do not wish to lend our aid and support to you this day, but that we are anxious not to over-burden you during this particularly busy and intense period. We are aware of your body's need for rest and also of the demanding schedule that you are working to at this time.

You have before you a weekend teaching, then rushing back for a meeting against the backdrop of organising a retreat and what will be demanded of you there to ensure its smooth running. On top of this you have your responsibilities to the publishing work that you have undertaken. So if we do not come immediately when you call on occasion, it is not because we seek to deprive you, rather that we desire not to add to your burdens. Our love for you is constant, and this is true whether or not our voice is present.

✡

I am still very busy. Malachi puts this in context.

Within life there are always opportunities to go beyond the confines of the senses and enter the realms of spirit. Thought and feeling are not of the senses; they are activated by the senses. If you were to take the senses away, thought and feeling would remain, albeit in a very introverted way; they would stay very close to spirit because they would not be stimulated by contact with the environment or other people. But stimulation is in itself a problem; it is as if thought and feeling become fascinated, almost obsessed, with the external world and cleave to it rather than to spirit. This is why in some spiritual disciplines the stimulation of the senses is lessened or removed, so that thought and feeling can respond more totally to the divine. But we advocate balance in all things; you are in the world, why should you not enjoy the world? What opportunity for learning and experiencing would there be without the senses, without free will? For is it not the relationship between the material world and the world of spirit that you are here to affect and to learn from?

✡

We are aware that there is a kind of trust that is built through familiarity, repetition and consistency, but there is also a level of trust that has to do with this rather difficult relationship between the individual and the spirit realm. If humankind were all able to trust more in the guidance of spirit, things would become much easier. It is like driving a car: you are the driver and spirit is with you, but spirit is also beyond you and has a greater perspective. We do not ask that you passively wait for spirit to take the wheel, but neither do we ask that you try to control events yourself, either individually or collectively. The relationship between man and spirit is a cooperative venture. Perhaps one of the more difficult challenges for humanity is to be cooperative, particularly when it involves something for which there is no immediate personal gain or reward. Remember, you are not seekers of truth alone, you are also actively sought by truth.

✡

Indecipherable, that is the language of the soul. It is as if you all have aliens from other planets riding on your shoulders. You love them and they love you but they do not speak your language, they do not even breathe the air that you breathe; but still they are you and you are they. What a strange creature the human being is! The trouble is that you think of yourself as the lower half of the partnership, hardly ever as the soul. Change places with your soul, imagine yourself to be the one who sits upon the shoulders of David and tell us, as soul, how you feel and how it is to be the soul.

I feel tears ... he works so hard ... the things he dislikes about himself are irrelevant to me ... I wish I could help him more ... He suffers but he has beautiful qualities, so solid, like a rock ... I wish he could see what I can see. When I look up there is such light, such beauty and peace. And when I look down ... his poor neck, it aches, so stiff from his toils.

You see how easy it is to speak with your soul? You are one, your soul is you and you are your soul, but your soul is more than you. Together and apart, it is life that joins you. Your consciousness can move so easily into your soul: has it not just done so, was your experience not real? Consciousness imbues all that you are and your consciousness can even move beyond your soul. There is no trick, nor do you have to meditate for years to achieve it; it is simple. Your consciousness can range through your past lives, can visit the various spheres and realms, can move also into the Causal plane – all you have to do is truly accept that it can, and it will.

✡

It is early, a spring morning; as I meditate I am drawn to the dawn birdsong outside my window, the church bell ringing at the top of the hill, beyond that the sound of a train in the distance and the constant hiss of London traffic ...

It is the world, the world of the senses is it not? This is where life starts, the home of the senses, so reassuring, so vibrant. And now move beyond the senses, become your soul as you did before and look up, look up to the light that you saw yesterday. That light is the light of the Higher Self, let yourself be drawn to it, feel it envelop you.

There is such a sense of lightness here ... of great expansiveness ... everything or everybody is aware of my presence and I am aware of theirs ... many greater than I ... but there is no judgment ... this is where I belong ... and it is where they belong too ... the foot does not curse the hand ... there is total acceptance ... I am one ... and I am many ... How odd.

And now look down my friend.

I see it all, but I feel no anguish at all, no anguish and no pain, just understanding; but it is more a feeling of understanding, that I could not readily render into words. I see it all, the joys and horrors of life and yet I, or perhaps I should say we, are absolutely still and calm.

And so you have your Higher Self; like a great department store of contentment, is it not?

✡

Up until now there has been the development of your ability to talk, to bring help and assistance through the spoken word. You are forty-seven today; perhaps this marks a transition onward, a new form of development in your work.

I see an intense vibrant green light with gold within it.

Christ consciousness comes like a soaring grace.

I feel as if I am on the edge of a great and majestic procession, unstoppable, eternal.

You cannot command it, it comes to those who wait, to those who are patient.

Surrounded by the gentle movements of angels' wings. I have never in my life imagined that something so very powerful could be so tender and gentle.

There is you, there is your self, there is your soul, there is your Higher Self, there is the Christos which embraces all. Beyond that, there is the unknowable God. Each is distinct from the other and yet dependent upon it.

✡

I heard somewhere that creation is a projection of the mind of the God within. This I can understand from an intellectual point of view, but I recall once in America, as a younger man, having to cut down some trees. As the axe bit into the wood, the smell of the pine resin, the shock up my arms; these things were so intense and so tangible, it is difficult to think of them as being produced from within and then projected out. If such things are projections then clearly there is some agreement about their nature, because my wife saw the same thing.

Incarnation is an agreement, a re-tuning of the frequency of your perception; when you are able to talk with me you re-tune the dial very slightly. We could say that the physical life is a part of their spectrum of perception, of the frequency range, but we feel that this would come as no surprise to you. What you are struggling with is not the understanding of these truths but their realisation; this is a different matter entirely. To realise the truth of creation, to make it a reality, means to accept it; this means a great insecurity for the ego, the lord of the material world. Some truths bring anxiety, they separate you from those things that you know and have come to rely upon. So this, we feel, is what is troubling you.

✡

I am feeling a little angry as I go into meditation this morning, so I try to put this out of my mind before I start.

Do not, do not ever lose your anger, talk yourself out of your anger, or feel that your anger should be set apart from yourself. Your anger stokes the fires that burn against injustice, against stupidity and against ignorance. Life would doubtless be a great deal more comfortable without it, but you are not here simply to resign yourself to what you see around you. You are here to see it and compare it to another truth, a truth that you carry deep within yourself.

Both Caesar and Deuteronomy [*the laws of the Old Testament*] have a specific place within the Holy Book [... *long pause* ...] What we wish to convey is sometimes limited by what you are prepared to accept, my son ... We are talking about the phenomenon of Law, those formless structures which are the matrix upon which creation is built. Many of these are uncovered and articulated in the Holy Book. Caesar made laws, Caesar called himself God (this is the meaning of the name) but Caesar was not God, he was man. At best the laws created by man reflect and embody the laws of creation, but not always; more often man-made laws seek to maintain a certain freedom of commerce, and within limits, freedoms for individuals; they are more often concerned with matters of social interaction.

The laws of creation do not disturb themselves with such issues; they concern themselves merely with harmony, with elegance. Those who are in tune with the laws of creation will not conflict with the laws of the land unless they choose it; the laws of creation are prior, prior even to man. So we have two levels, the laws of man, of Caesar, and the Laws of creation represented in the Book of Deuteronomy; sometimes they are in tune, sometimes not. So what is the relationship between them and how will you know which is which, for do you not live in Caesar's world?

The relationship between the two, their relative relationship, can be understood in many ways, in the understanding of beauty for example. When the human is in alignment with spiritual laws the result will be beautiful and his or her capacity to appreciate beauty will be enhanced. Where beauty does not exist and ugliness prevails, there perhaps we must question whether these two realms are in harmony. Anger is also an indicator: when you feel angry at the behaviour of another perhaps you can question whether their behaviour is in alignment with the creative laws. Should you look behind that anger we suspect that you will find pain, the pain of a soul that knows harmony, that knows beauty, that knows justice and tolerance – a soul that looks out upon a world that can sometimes be filled with ugliness, with injustice, with disharmony and with intolerance. Here the soul communicates, strives to present a different perspective, using the language of feeling.

So in a world where truth is treated as a commodity for the convenience of the individual, how can you best use the opportunity that life presents, how can you make a conscious link between the world of the living and the spirit world? One way is to trust your anger, trust your passion, trust the beauty that makes your heart ache with rage and longing: this, as much as anything else, is the voice of your soul.

✡

I have a friend who is very old and very ill. He wants to die and yet it seems as though death keeps cheating him. It is difficult to see the purpose in such suffering.

When I walked the earth I, too, lived to a very old age. I lived long enough to suffer the indignities of a failing body, long enough for my eyes and my mind to dim and become feeble, long enough to feel the ache in my limbs that never ceased. Like you I would ask, 'Why? Is this reward I get for the life I have spent? To suffer in misery and solitude? How long must this twilight go on before I am allowed to surrender to the night?'

It went on and on, for a good many years. But even these years were not wasted, no; still there was learning. I had always been a strong man, very self-willed. To be reduced in such a way was a terrible thing to me. Better to be struck down whilst standing than to suffer such a weakening, I had always felt – but it was precisely this reduction, the very thing I feared, that I had to endure in order to learn.

To be utterly dependent on other people is not easy. It is not easy but it is a reality that is true for all, true for all and accepted by few. None of us can live without the assistance of others and what more direct way to learn this than in old age and illness? As we surrender to the care of those people who surround us there is so much to learn about human nature; those small kindnesses that are shown by some become so important, reveal the goodness of their spirit. Then there are those that are incapable of showing such kindness; none can hide their true nature from the ill and infirm. As they help the aged, so the elderly help them to become aware of their strengths and limitations.

It is all a preparation for letting go into the arms of the next life. When a young, strong person is deprived of life due to an accident or fatal illness they have far, far more difficulty adjusting to the afterlife. The shock, all the hopes, the unfulfilled expectations, the loved ones, the attachments that have to be let go. They have a far more difficult time than those who have gradually moved towards the end, those for whom passing is a blessed relief from a life that has been fulfilled.

It is not always immediately apparent what lessons the soul desires to learn from life, but they are there and everything that you have lived through you have lived through to enable that learning, that fulfilment, to take place. When you finally look back on your life from the vastness of that which awaits you, you will see clearly why it has been the way that it has, the importance of every step and every day. You will see that nothing has been wasted, nothing has been for no reason.

Eventually you will see where your life fits within the great scheme – that life is no more than the blink of an eye, a brief moment in an ocean of timelessness, a glance away from the valley of peace that is your true home, from whence you came and to which you will return.

✡

Several days later Malachi offered this.

Ultimately we are all pitched into that great unknown. No matter how small or great, none can avoid it; but my, what a surprise awaits the person who makes that passage! There is no death; would you be talking to us if there were? We think not. There is no death; the soul lives on and it is the body that is left behind. Anybody who has ever seen a body after death, that of a loved one or even a beloved pet, knows that everything that made it what it was has gone, all that is left is the shell. But where does that vital life force go? Does it dissipate into the air like steam from a kettle? No it does not; it retains its integrity in another form, it moves into another dimension, very, very slightly out of coincidence with your own, and there it is introduced to its new life. It really is like a new birth, attended by all those who were important to that soul who have gone before. Then, like a new-born infant, it must learn how to live in this new world, without the encumbrance of an old, perhaps sick, body. If the illness that caused death was particularly painful or traumatic a long healing sleep may ensue – not to heal the body, no, but to heal the soul.

On waking, the life is reviewed; but now in the context of the soul's purpose, all the relevant lifetimes that led to the one just passed are recalled. Then the effects of every action or inaction within that life are understood, and the work of forgiveness begins. There is no wrathful God to punish sinners; God does not have a choice, is only capable of love. The work of forgiveness is from the self to the self; it is a challenge of reconciliation and understanding that may take a very long time.

With help and understanding from those who have gone before, consciousness gradually expands, through the spheres, through the layers of wisdom around the earth, until the individual soul recognises his or her place within the Higher Self that sent it forth. When this happens it is a beautiful reunion, like a baby looking into the eyes of its mother for the first time, seeing the light of love shining there and remembering why it was born. So do not fear death: it is the culmination of life. Just as a pollen-laden bee return to the hive, the place where it belongs, so humanity ultimately returns to the Creator, the place where we belong.

✡

This little passage came after I had neglected my meditations for some time. Not because I was busy, but because I was depressed and resentful about the whole process. It really was a difficult time; I felt that my writing had no value, I was just making it all up. Finally, one morning I was drawn to meditate despite my resistance and in the meditation I experienced a profound release.

Experience has shown that even when you are not in conscious dialogue with spirit, it still surrounds you. Your guides and teachers still reach out towards you. Human consciousness is such a strange thing, quite unparalleled. Its inherent quality, the ability to focus, is also that which keeps it from perceiving other realms. Now Yeshua wishes to speak with you.

My brother, long and deep is the darkness of the soul. It wraps around your shoulders like a heavy, dusty, burdensome cloak; choking you, blinding your eyes and your heart to what is around you. Yet every laboured step that you have taken with that garment on your back has been taken with me by your side. Now, as you cast it off and step once more into the light I walk with you still, your friend, your companion, I never left you, I never will.

And so it comes to pass. And you are left wondering as you look back why this did not happen weeks, months, years ago. But life is not like that: things happen when they can, when you are able, and not a minute before.

In every person there is a wholeness or completeness, but it is like a cutting from a plant, a rose not grown or come to bloom in its own right, it is not yet proved. If you watch a rose grow, become strong, put forth blooms and fruit through the seasons and the years and then die, then you see an essence that has been proved. That rose grew according to its essential nature, it fulfiled its essential nature; it put forth blossom, fruit and seed and then died, which is also part of its essential nature. Now we would apply this to your relationship to spirit and to your spiritual guides. You were born with an essence within you, a cutting from the whole, with the knowledge that at some point in the future you would have the potential to connect with spirit in the way that you are now doing.

Each time you speak to a new guide such as Josephes or myself, you make that potential real. When you write it down or put it forward for publishing it becomes part of the public domain, like the flowers and fruit of the rose. Now in essence Josephes, Malachi, Little Cloud, Adolphus, Llane and Yeshua have all walked beside you, some more closely, some at a greater distance. We have all walked beside you and you have taken each one of us to your heart and, to some extent, integrated our presence; at least you recognise our distinct tone or note. By allowing us to influence your life, by giving voice to our words, you have planted new plants. This we appreciate very deeply.

Now within your meditations there is a new voice, new yet old and familiar. Yeshua will never come more than occasionally, and then only when he wishes it. He is the most beautiful rose in your garden ... Listen well to his words, write them with care. His words have the potential not just of planting a rose but of seeding a garden. It is there still, not so very far beneath the layers of man's neglect. In time the garden of Eden will re-emerge, tended by the Children of Light, and far more beautiful than anything that has gone before.

✡

In your imagination take a small pebble in your hand and make your way down to the sea. Children love to throw pebbles into the sea, it has always been so. Perhaps they like to see their little splash in amongst the great waves that roll onto the beach. Or perhaps it is more symbolic – a way of having a connection with the sea. The ocean, like spirit, is eternal. It is as near to a living eternity as you will find on this planet. Give yourself to spirit, cast your pebble into the water; it is a good feeling is it not? But what happens to that feeling tomorrow or the day after? Does it affect your life and actions then?

You are not children, and casting a pebble is not enough for adults, no. So many think that feeling good, praying and doing good deeds is enough to develop spiritually, or that reading books such as this one will make them wise. It will not. It takes hard work to develop spiritually, and most of that work has to be done in your ordinary relationships with other people. The inhibition of those things that prevent empathy and sharing, this is the work of spiritual development.

✡

I have been working very hard just lately and I am having to fight to stay awake during my morning meditations.

When I was alive the experience of my life showed me that it was not possible to keep on and on without rest, without reaching for a source greater than myself. Everybody needs their source. Everybody needs somewhere, someone, to whom they can turn, someone greater than themselves, with that little bit more perspective. Father Abraham needs his source, even God needs a source, and now your source, Yeshua, wishes for a moment of your time.

You wonder, my brother, why it is that I come on this day? There is never a day when I am not with you, for my light is the vestment of the world. There are none who do not walk within it; like the wings of a great angel I enfold the world in gentleness and in peace. But so many do not feel what I give; their fears and worries blind them to my love and even I cannot help them open their eyes. I feel their questing in times of crisis or profound peace, when they momentarily open to my presence, and I feel their denial and their cynicism like a knife when they turn away. But not all turn away; there are those that stop and let my light in. They may not recognise who brings it but they open to it and in that opening are healed. It is such as these, the meek and the humble, who recognise that they need help, who make my pitiful task worthwhile. So do not ever think that I have left or forsaken you. I will not, I cannot, I am here.

✡

It is I, Malachi. Accept nothing that does not fit your own deeper understanding. There are many explanations but only one truth, and the truth is good. People do not accept it because they fear it; they fear it because they feel that it is opposed to their survival, their autonomy and their sovereignty. But it is not. Imagine a simple basket in the possession of a small uneducated community. For many years this wondrous object is passed from family to family, each one marvelling at its mystery, the beauty of the weaving, the shape and the form; it is admired, decorated, celebrated.

Then one day somebody realises that it is actually for carrying things and wishes to use it for this. Imagine the liberation that some will feel in recognising its true purpose, the fear and anger that others will feel at having their prized object removed from the rituals and traditions they have built around it. You understand? The truth can set you free but it does this through the destruction of ignorance. The truth liberates, it bring peace and understanding. But at the same time it destroys. It destroys the fear, ignorance and doubt that bind humanity to illusion.

✡

I am at an Anglican retreat centre where we have our annual psychotherapy training retreat. At this moment it is very early morning and I am sitting meditating in the graveyard of the parish church, an exquisite 11th-century building. The birds are singing and the sun is coming up over the trees, warming the soft honey-coloured stone. It is quite beautiful and I am aware of how much my identity as an Englishman is tied up with scenes like this, of English village life.

What we see is how religion has taken root in your culture, so far from the culture which we knew. We see what has been assimilated along the way, the Pagan, the Druidic and the Roman, the testaments and rituals of the Middle East – such diversity from one simple message.

I look around at the yew trees, the gravestones, the chrysanthemums on the graves, the soft grass and the gravel paths. If the Christos is to reassert itself what will become of all this, that is so precious to the history of this country? I look at the clergymen who are sharing the centre with us at this time, so well meaning but ...

They are the old guard, and some among them are very fine souls indeed. The Church as you know it will not disappear completely; some of the rituals will be revised, some of the buildings will be put to other uses. Spirit is not a revolutionary force in the destructive sense; it builds on what has gone before, it does not replace it. Look at the evidence around you: the urns on the graves are modelled on those from Greece and Rome, the shell of Aphrodite is set in the church wall, the yews are from pagan times. Each new and great teaching embraces what has gone before; it does not polarise with the status quo. This is all in accordance with the law, and so it will be with the teachings of Christ. It cannot be any other way; this is how history is formed. So do not fear the loss of those things you love about your country, that make it what it is. They will be reawakened to their true purpose, that is all.

✡

'There is a green hill far away without the City wall, where our dear Lord was crucified, who died to save us all ...' The words come spontaneously into my head and often precede Malachi's speech. This was a favourite hymn when I was a boy at school, when I could sing my heart out with no shame or embarrassment at all.

It is rather too late for you to say, 'I have not been meditating these past few weeks therefore I have not been involved in development, in my spiritual path.' It (not meditating) is all part of your spiritual path, my son. The spiritual path is not a straight path; your passage along it moves like a pendulum, swinging off in one direction and then off in the other, never walking directly along it, only crossing it. But we rejoice at this renewed dialogue all the same. We look forward to this time each morning when we can commune and help you understand your path and the development you will need to complete before the end of the year. Farewell for now my son.

✡

New Year's Eve

Another New Year, another cycle complete, a time to look back and reflect on your progress over the year, and having done so to look forward to the upcoming year, to the improvements, to the plans and hopes for yourself, your work and your loved ones. But there are greater cycles too, great wheels of time that take thousands of years to come full turn, and the greater cycle within which this year has moved is now almost completed too.

Every single action that is taken by humankind sends ripples across the surface of time, and these ripples are visited again and again throughout the cycles – visited personally, nationally and globally. Now, as this great cycle comes to a close, humanity is revisiting the most important event in the history of this planet bar none: never before and never again will God walk among you in the shape of an individual man.

The Millennium is not arbitrary; it marks exactly one age, two thousand years since the birth of Christ. For the next few years, as he establishes his presence in the hearts of humankind his energy will be felt as never before. It will bring such peace to those who can accept it, such healing to those who are open to it. Look forward, look for the gentle, pearlescent gold that is the colour of the Christ.

✡

Interspersed between the days and nights, the moments of time, is timelessness. Time is a fabrication built within a great sea of timelessness, constant and yet unstable. Without it there would be no movement. And what do we have in the realms of spirit to rival this phenomenon? We have the ever-present now, and that ever-present now is loaded with the vastness of knowing. So our sense of movement comes not from looking across or along a time line forward or back, it comes from contemplating the vaults of knowledge and understanding that exist around and within us. These vaults are not full of books or even words as you know them. The knowledge within them is held within certain frequencies; these can be seen spiritually as colour. Each of the colours has meaning, and the complexity of meaning is denoted by how the colours blend, their vibrancy and juxtaposition. The human aura is full of colour which indicates the purpose and qualities of the individual.

✡

One of your qualities is to be able to accept what comes towards you without fighting it; the pink in your aura enables this. You move into a new situation and you accept what is given in that situation. Others, particularly those among the blue and purple, are more concerned with how things should be than how they are. To them you can appear almost passive, uninterested in what fires them. To you they appear to be unable to work with what is presented to them; they are always changing it, qualifying or placing conditions. So here you have some of the qualities of the colours that are in individuals' auras.

With the reds you will seldom find judgement; they too, accept what comes. With the blues and purples it is more a case of seeing how things can be and getting frustrated with how they are. The yellows and golds are very accepting of what they see, but their vision is more intuitive than practical. They see the spiritual vision, but it is very hard for them to translate this into action or plans. They are the idealists, and because of this they can sometimes cling to the past and be quite inflexible. With the greens, they see to the heart of the matter; they can create equilibrium amongst all the others, but only if they feel safe within themselves, within their environment; they are like sea creatures, darting away at the first sign of danger. All the colours have qualities and all the qualities have their limitations. You would not ask a pilot to perform surgery, but would you not trust your life to both surgeon and pilot in their own area of expertise?

✡

Good Friday

In reality the crucifixion and resurrection did not take place in the spring, any more than the birth of Christ was at midwinter. But given that this is the time when the crucifixion and resurrection are celebrated, all conform to this and those energies are most accessible both in the temporal world and the world of spirit at this time of year. To explain exactly the date of the crucifixion is not in our power. Even if it were we would not commit ourselves; so many otherwise brilliant and accurate channellings have been dismissed by the public because of a difference of one or two days when compared with another. What we can say is that it took place not long after the time of year when Yeshua was born, which was late summer. So it would be in the winter time, with perhaps the same gap between birth and death as that between Christmas and Easter.

✡

I have an old caravan by a lake in West Sussex. I often come here with just the dog for company as a retreat from home and my work. I am staying for a few days.

I am here.

And so am I. It is always a pleasure to speak with you when you are more relaxed, doing those things that you love to do, that give you respite from the pressures of your work and family. This place has a delightful energy, a soft, calming effect due to the body of water. Earth, air, fire and water [*I always cook over a charcoal brazier at the caravan*], all are brought together in this place, and when you come here you can be in perfect relationship with the four elements. This is so unusual in your modern life, and yet it is so necessary to partake of those simple things which God gave rather than those which man has created out of what was given. It is our hope that if man does not destroy himself first, he will one day return to the simplicity of such pleasures as this.

✡

People love their holidays, but why should pleasure be so polarised with work? It is only attitude that makes it so. Why should not work reflect those things that people find important and enjoyable? In every lifetime opportunities come around in cycles; in every age they repeat. You have only to see and respond, to make those opportunities into reality. They are there, constantly presenting themselves, it is only your expectations that confound them.

Expect nothing and nothing will become your friend. You will have no disappointments, but do you really want to make a friend of nothing? Nothing is rather a cool companion. At the same time you know the dangers of making your hopes for the future too concrete. If what you want is a red coat then this can blind you to all the blue coats, the greens, the yellows, the mackintoshes, even the capes, umbrellas and blankets that may come your way.

On the other hand if you simply empty your mind and wait for what life may bring in your direction, then perhaps waiting will become your cause and you will miss the opportunity when it comes. Somewhere between these two poles there is a dynamic, a position of open-minded expectation, informed by a sense of your own purpose and direction. Not to such a degree that it excludes change, and not so loose that it disenables any action. It truly is a point of tension, an attitude of awareness, both inner and correspondingly outer. You must describe your general direction. To say that you are heading north is perhaps better than saying exactly which road and footpath you will travel. North can respond to your need in many ways, but roads and footpaths are fixed.

✡

I am the way, the truth and the light. What a beautiful and elegant teaching. Think of the 'I', a simple vertical line that connects above with below, heaven and earth, God and soul, soul and man. Think of the 'am', a proclamation and celebration of existence. The connection between God and man exists. I AM the evidence, I AM the proof. Language was not created by scientists; they use it to prove their points but they did not create it. Language was a gift from God, handed to the ancient scholars. The syllables and sounds are not words, they are vibrations, each one formed from the breath of God, each one mimicking the act of creation itself and creating in its turn a new pattern, a new reality. Think about affirmations: they are not just words; some have a very deep meaning buried within them. Think about the one so often used by Yeshua.

> I
> I am
> I am the way

Think about that. The I, that which connects heaven and earth is the Way.

> I am the way, the truth.

That which connects heaven and earth is the source of truth.

> I am the way the, truth and the life.

That which connects heaven and earth, that slender figure that represents the very core of our identity is the source of all life. I am the way, the truth and the life. I am the road home and the road that leads from. All things emerge from I, all things return to I. I am irrefutable, constant and eternal. I will. I will never die.

✡

Experience in the place that you now occupy is not easy. It is like the desert where nothing grows and the major preoccupation is surviving the cold of the night and the heat of the day. The desert appears to be such a godforsaken place, but it is not God who forsakes the desert but man himself. It is not possible for God to love one part of his creation any more or less than another, however much man may claim it or want it to be so. The love of the Creator is constant; what constantly changes is man's relationship to this love. How would man know love if he did not also experience its absence? He leaves home; he turns back; he knows his home because he spends time in the desert, and he knows that he is in the desert because it does not feel like his home. What can you do but wait? If the nature of creation is to change and the nature of the Creator is constancy within that change, then it stands to reason that what swings one way will eventually swing another.

There is nothing, not one thing, nor any person, that can bring assistance to those who do not recognise their need. Need is like a door through which spiritual love can pass. There were those who turned their back on Yeshua; they walked away, they gained nothing. To them he was just a stupid man, egotistical, making ludicrous claims. They dismissed him and were none the wiser. Yeshua said, 'Blessed are the meek', and who are the meek? The meek are those who have recognised their failings, who know that they are empty without God. Life has brought them to that place in themselves where they know that without the love of God they are nothing, dust upon the ground. These are the meek.

Extend beyond the limits of time and space, which form after all, a tiny speck within a much larger reality. You await our touch; expectant, you think, 'Is that thought reliable? Is that image from me or does it come from somewhere else? Is that the voice that I am seeking or is it just my mind wandering?' It all comes from you, but we come from that greatly expanded version of yourself that includes so much more than you can be aware of in any given moment. It includes the greater part of who you are, all that which exists beyond the veil of time and space. So do not concern yourself with what comes from where. If you discriminate too much at the beginning you will lose the connection; let it flow.

Experience within the spirit spheres is quite different from that upon the planet. We transmit to you those things that are on our agenda, but this is not enough to fill the hours that you spend in meditation. It is not really within the remit of spirit to take initiative in relation to humanity; we must wait until you ask. But sometimes there is this stand-off between yourself and ourselves, each of us waits passively for the other. Sometimes your meditations might be more productive if you could frame questions that you need to ask. There are many things that you could bring to us. Questions that your clients ask, your own questions, all these things we can respond to in our way. Many of them you may feel we have already responded to, for we do talk, we do influence your thinking whilst you are in dialogue with others. But here we are thinking more for the purpose of writing down some of the perspectives that we have to offer, of speaking those things while you have your tape recorder turned on, so that you can then transcribe them. Bring us questions. Do not concern yourself about what you already know on the subject; bring the questions to us and we will either repeat ourselves for the purpose of transcription or we will bring fresh light to bear on the subject, but we can do none of this unless you bring us your questions.

✡

In every person there is the intention to do well, to fulfil a life's purpose, and nobody is born with a purpose that is evil. Purpose is neither good nor ill. Usually that which must be met, overcome, learned from and brought into the harbour of the heart is very obviously there amongst the family – parents, children, brothers and sisters, the circumstances of birth, or a trait within the individual. It is highly unlikely that a soul purpose would demand that one individual dominate a nation and put thousands to death. It is in the interpretation of the message of the soul that these sorts of plans are conceived and executed. You may well ask, 'If the needs of the soul are so simple then why is there so much pain and deviancy within the world?' It is very difficult to answer this, but deviancy begets deviancy, certain attitudes and beliefs that are accepted in the world are father to similar beliefs in the new and the young.

The soul is a small voice, the clamour of the world is loud, and not all souls are aware of the loving guidance of spirit, not all souls are aware of that which begat them. They have a sense of purpose, a very general sense of purpose, but it is nebulous, diffuse. This is why spiritual guidance is so important, it can help those souls that are lost to establish a sense of direction, a sense of connectedness with God. There is nothing in creation that can bring a sense of meaning to life like the touch of spirit. Nothing can equal the feeling of peace and stillness that comes from the breath of spirit. Nothing.

Chapter 3

The nature of mind

It is with pleasure that we welcome you back to your morning meditations after your brief holiday, and it is with pleasure that we find you rested. Stress, as you know, is the enemy of meditation and relaxation is its friend. When you are relaxed you allow those things to flow into your mind that we wish to communicate, but when you are stressed your mind darts about seeking solutions and listening only to that which will bring immediate relief from the suffering of stress. On the other hand, just as stress is the enemy of meditation so the converse is true, meditation is the enemy of stress. It is very difficult to move from a stressed state to a relaxed state when the pressures of the world are intense. The candle helps, and so does your chanting of the Aum. And you have your own methods, your morning bath; very often when we cannot reach you in meditation we find that you are perfectly open to us when you are submerged in hot water. Spirit seldom arrives in the centre of the eye, it is when you are not looking for it that you can see it best, in your peripheral vision. We would suggest also the use of visualisation, taking any scene in the tranquillity of nature, particularly those involving green foliage and water, is always extremely helpful in combating stress.

✡

There is only one department in life that requires more attention than any other and that department is the mind. The mind, over all other things, is that which so often suffers the neglect of humanity and yet it is there, connected to God, connected to all things. How you think is ultimately how you will be. It is the mind, the thought processes, that create the moulds into which the metal of life is poured. It is the mind that creates the shapes, the architecture, the plans. It is the mind that designs first in pictures and images, that sees roads through land that has none, health where disease has been and disease where health has been. It is the mind that shapes the future or holds on to the past.

The mind is primary, the first formation, it is that which determines tomorrow. As long as what is envisaged is within the laws of the universe the mind can form it, not instantly but eventually. If people really accepted the truth about their minds they would not treat them so lightly, use them to make excuses, rationalise and plot. It is like setting a tiger to pull a plough. The mind of man is they the same substance as the mind of God, all that divides them is their proximity to the source.

✡

In the eyes of the superstitious person things are either good or bad. In the eyes of the educated person all things contain both good and bad. It is not the thing that is inherently good or bad but the use to which it is put. Objects and events cannot make choices; even the most refined animals can only make the most rudimentary of choices, and even then they do not have a conscience to guide them. It is choice, free will, that creates issues of good and bad and this falls within the province of man. With man and man alone comes choice. With choice comes action; with action comes consequence; and with consequence comes responsibility. Actions are gauged as either good or bad depending the degree of responsibility the individual is prepared to take for those actions.

But the world is not neatly divided into good and bad, right and wrong, no matter how man might wish it so. Creation is not a series of polarities in the eyes of God. In the mind of God the world is simply a hierarchy of love, in which some things are closer to the source than others.

✡

If you observe yourself as you sit expounding upon this subject or that, you will notice that you frequently come to a hiatus. You run out of ideas and things to say, as if the breath has all been expelled from your lungs, and there is a moment's pause before you breathe in again. But what do you breathe in and from where does it come? As you gulp the air it is like accessing a vast, living encyclopedia that is not entirely in your control. Who amongst the scientists and philosophers on the earth can explain this, the simplest and the most obvious question? 'Ah.' they say, 'but the mind is a mysterious thing, nobody really knows how it works.'

The mind is an energy field, many-layered, many-faceted. It is a field that encompasses both God and humanity, the whole of the planet too. It is both universal and particular, and potentially you can tune into any part of it. Imagine a room: a kettle is boiling on the hob and the room is filled with steam. The steam is like the mind, it is in contact with the entire contents of the room. On one wall hangs a crucifix, on another, a picture of a popular singer. On the bookshelf is a copy of the Koran, against the wall, a television set. Magazines and newspapers are strewn on the table and there is a telephone and a radio. In the corner is a cat curled up and there are people in the room. Objects, symbols and history, other species – the steam embraces them all.

Here and there in the room, where there is something cooler, something of a different temperature, the steam condenses and there are droplets of water. Now this is very much how the mind works when you sit in meditation or talk with another person. Where there is a different vibration from that of the mass of mind, and discussion and thought create this different vibration, the droplets condense into thoughts and ideas and words. Out of that great field of unformed energy that contains everything, those droplets condense, drip into your consciousness and inform what you think and say. Some people dwell in the corner of the room, some can stride across it imbibing wisdom from everywhere, but the principle is the same.

✡

We will tell you something. Do not think that when you pass from life to spirit everything will suddenly become easier. If you analyse your life and the things that disturb and distress you, what is behind many of them a feeling of loss, a distant memory of the Creator, a longing for God. Once you are in spirit you do not have life to help distract you from this; the longing for God will pierce your heart like a dagger of love. So live your life, meet the challenges it presents with joy; these challenges are solid, moist and visceral. In spirit we do not have this privilege, there is less to separate the soul from its goal; with no time, no space, we have only mind, only the eternal now. How we long for the return of our lives; how we long for the reunion with God! Rejoice in your life, whatever it brings.

✡

Chapter 4

The process of inspired channelling

This chapter is made up of Malachi's comments about how and why he is speaking to me. The mechanism and purpose of our relationship. In this morning's meditation I feel as if I am wearing a hat. I don't know if this is due to activity in my crown chakra or if this is Malachi perhaps trying to indicate something.

It is a hat of sorts. In the very hot sun in the time when I lived, I could not do without some form of covering for my head. People who went into the blazing heat of the day without covering for their heads would very soon succumb to heat stroke. Now I am the covering for your head. If you were to expose yourself directly to the energy of God, you would probably go mad and die; the human does not mix easily with the divine. So I mediate that energy to you, on behalf of your Higher Self. When you feel this pressure, this tingling around the top of your head, you will know that we are seeking an audience, that we are humbly requesting an opportunity to speak with you, to bring peace, to bring succour and to bring the truth.

✡

Out-of-this-world experiences, such as what you are experiencing now, as you speak words into a tape recorder believing them to come from the dead, are not out of our world. For your world is simply a capsule, a sphere within ours. We do not know everything, but our position in spirit enables us to have a different perspective to your own, not always easy to put into words. The further from the worlds of incarnation that we progress, the closer we come to our ultimate goal, which is God. The closer we come to God the less we are able to translate our experience and knowledge into earthly language. It is as if there is a crossover point in progression, a river once traversed that cannot be returned over. Still we try, and where words fail us we send clusters of direct understanding to you, like coloured crystals that dissolve when dropped in water, leaving threads and trails of brilliance behind them, which you can then contemplate and interpret in your own time.

✡

Continuing from our discussion yesterday: it is not really intended that these spheres overlap. Your world and my world are discrete from one another because the experiences and opportunities for learning available within them are different. It would be extremely confusing to try to live two experiences at the same time. Having said this, they do overlap from time to time, for example when a great soul incarnates, or during meditation, inspiration or channelling. Then there are usually quite profound effects. You have seen this with your first book. Although it is a story from a different time from that within your own particular sphere, it concerns, through your writing about Josephes and Yeshua, material from another sphere. When spheres overlap in this way it always brings forth extreme reactions. When you think of the range of responses and reactions to your words in the short time since they were published: tears, anger, indifference ... Some have been deeply moved and others highly critical and cynical. There will be opposition; it is as well that you learn about this and learn to have confidence in your work. This your best protection.

✡

Truly there is but one way forward, you must take your convictions in your hands, not holding them as a secret that feeds only yourself but with open hands, so that others can see and decide if they wish to partake of what you have to offer. We speak here not specifically to you, my son, but to all who seek and walk the spiritual path. You are here to feed the hungry, not just to feed yourselves. Spirit gives you the nourishment to do this. Do not give from your own supply but from that which we give you, and there will always be plenty; you will have no need to fear poverty.

Within every intent we can never be sure how the effects will work out in the physical realms. Once a particular plan or idea is launched we can only watch the wave of energy, can only observe its progress; we can only adjust the direction by giving advice, and this only works if our advice is listened to by those who are able to affect the outworkings of the wave. It is like delivering a message to the doors of a palace. We know that the king is in there, but not exactly where, and so we speak the message to the doorman. How the king will get the message, in what way, from whom and when, is unknown to us. It is up to those who live in the palace. Every member of humankind is like a palace. Take the message, guard it, but do not let the guardianship stop the light falling from it. Give it, but do not let the giving dilute it. It is more precious than gold and more common than soil.

✡

Maximise your growth potential by ceasing to hesitate when you are speaking your inspirations. The words form, and they hang in your mind while you consider them and evaluate them before you commit them to voice or paper. If you can remove this stage of evaluation, you will then be speaking directly; it will be as if your tongue and ours are one. You will have to trust, you will have to have faith, because you will no longer be able to stop and consider whether this is spiritual or whether it is from your own past: But we say this: for you this consideration is irrelevant; you cannot separate yourself from your soul. The fact that much of your soul is unconscious to you does not make its existence any less real. Let the words flow. You do this all the time and you pay it no mind, but you do not do it when you sit down in the early morning to set about your daily meditation. This is the time when the words should flow, and yet it is the time when you apply more critical discrimination than at any other time. So speak into your tape recorder and be damned! Decide what to do with what has been spoken after it has been recorded, not before.

✡

This morning we feel your dissatisfaction with what we are giving you. It is not within the remit of those who presently talk to you to go too far beyond the type of material that we are currently imparting. We are bound by the protocols and laws that appertain to the enlightenment we have gained, and there are those we have to answer to as well.

Well, with no disrespect intended at all, I am often left with the impression that there is much more that is not being made available, that I am not gaining access to.

There is a great deal more, not all of which has to come directly from us. In meditation you can access many different realms. The corridors within the spirit world are long, the chambers are vast, and all are hung with the most opulent pictures and tapestries. But these pictures are not oil paintings and neither are they tapestries woven from silk; they are living, they can be entered, they can be experienced. Each one is a living cell of experience and wisdom. You can walk these corridors, my son, and you can enter these realms.

OK. I am walking down a long corridor – in fact I am reminded of the corridors of the Uffizi Gallery in Florence, hung with the paintings of the great masters. Malachi is here, dressed in robes; we are walking; the ceiling is very high. To my left and to my right as we walk are vivid pictures, each picture filled with colour and tone and light. Some I am quite repelled by, and some I am quite drawn to. There is one which is a sort of turquoise green that I am very attracted to. I enter. It is incredibly still here, still and quiet. I feel as if I am absorbing this colour through my skin, through my pores, it seems very balancing to my own energy. Even in my physical body as I sit and meditate I can see the colour behind my eyes and I can feel myself surrounded by it so clearly. OK, I come out again and into the corridor. Malachi is still here.

This corridor is in fact an interface between the human and the spiritual that is lodged within the spirit realm. You could just as easily visualise being surrounded by the colour of your choice. The effect would be much the same, but it is so much more acceptable when spiritual truth is clothed in the images and the language of the earth, is it not? It is very difficult to imbibe the riches of a realm that is not of the human, very difficult for man to imagine what he has never seen. If you were to imagine going to another planet: perhaps their most precious commodity is something that is unrecognisable to you, and they bring this substance as an offering, as a gift to their honoured guest. You would look at it and wonder what it was for, what to do with it. You would accept it and take it home; perhaps you would put it on the mantelpiece and say to your friends, 'Yes this was a gift from the citizens of such and such a planet,' but still you would not give it the credit that they would – how could you?

It is the same when you visit the realms of spirit. Of course there is more, and each time you come you swim in it, but it is difficult to understand the value of what you are receiving if you do not recognise it in its pure state. This is why the image of a corridor hung with beautiful works of art and the association with myself make the experience more acceptable to the mind. It is better to quietly receive, quietly absorb, give thanks and go on your way. The understanding will come later.

Yeshua was an expert at clothing the magnificent in the language of the mundane, and of course he used parable, stories, to do this. The simple stories he told took on a spiritual dimension, a depth of meaning that people carried away with them and remembered. Even now, after two thousand years, his teachings and sayings are as fresh and relevant as they were when they were spoken. He located the spiritual in the hearts of mankind by speaking as a man, in the language of man, but the message was from God.

✡

During meditation this morning a new 'teacher' stepped forward using rather arcane language. I took this as a lesson in discipline and discrimination.

New Voice: A good notion to bring in at this point is the issue of outside assistance. With people such as the ones that you are thinking of, the colophon [*the tail piece in old books giving the name of the printer, nowadays placed at the beginning of the volume*] has atrophied. I would advise you to lead them to a higher calling. You must realise that not all that is achieved is done through the offices of the teacher who now communicates with you in your meditations.

Who are you?

I am Kashar.

So you are not directly involved with the Malachi?

Not directly, but this makes me no less spiritual. I am soul just as he is soul; there is no difference between us.

With all due respect Kashar, I will stick with the teacher I have.

Malachi: And there you have it. Kashar is spirit, Kashar is an aspect of your own Higher Self. Why did you reject him?

Because I sensed his rigidity, a certain pride perhaps. His agenda seemed more personal than purposeful.

Your mind is a wonderful instrument, it can tune in to broadcasts from any aspect of your Higher Self in any language; but these languages, the aspects from which they come, may only vaguely know of the existence of one another or, depending on their progression, they may even misunderstand each other. It is the same in spirit as it is on earth. There are infinite sources of information within the Higher Self. It could be said that within the spirit realm the Higher Self is a vast array of repositories of wisdom. Some is relevant to your current life, some is not. Some complements your work, some does not.

To understand this distinction it is necessary to understand the chronology of incarnation, the expansion of consciousness over time. When the Buddha came, he brought teachings which were necessary and appropriate to the people of that time. When Christ came he brought teachings that were necessary and appropriate to the people of his time. When Babaji walked the earth he was teaching appropriately to his time. It is the same within the Higher Self: not all that step forward to speak know what you are involved in or why; unless they have achieved mastery they will bring the wisdom of their time. Remember, even in spirit all is not necessarily one, nor will it be for a good time to come.

Those teachings that remain within the consciousness of humanity are to some extent teachings that were appropriate to their time. In addition to this, each one of these teachers had a particular and distinct relationship to the Creator that was to help them to fulfil their purpose. The light that informs your path has to do with the Christ, and with the prophet Elijah and Father Abraham. Without these two, together with Joseph of Arimathea, the Christ could not have incarnated. This path is distinct, not better or worse – just distinct.

✡

Two weeks without contact with Malachi. It's always the same when I have a great deal of work to do; the focus of my attention slips away from the spiritual and becomes all the things I have to organise. My meditations are invaded by lists of jobs instead of Malachi's words.

Every time we approach there is a gamble, a gamble that is not based upon the laws of chance but upon the laws of free will. Man is like a set of scales, with the spiritual side of his nature in one pan and the material in the other. At certain times the material takes predominance, at others the spiritual takes predominance, and on some occasions the pans are more or less evenly balanced. For several weeks now your work has made your meditation difficult. When we find this state of affairs we do not force the issue and neither do you.

This morning we found the scales in almost perfect balance. As we approached we were aware that things could have gone either way, our approach could have tipped the material side or the spiritual side of your nature into greater predominance. It cannot be helped, and we know that you are aware of this. Now we have re-established contact with you in this way we are content to leave well alone.

On other occasions we come forward to greet you and although you could, you do not grasp the hand that is offered. Imagine your realm and ours to be like water and air, it is like a pool, with you beneath the water looking up at the surface, waiting for the hand to reach down towards you. Your thoughts are like leaves floating on the surface of the water, a little part of each one penetrating beneath the surface, and you scrutinise each as it passes, saying to yourself, 'No, it is debris, it is not what I am looking for.' So you do not take it, you do not grasp it. But who casts those leaves upon the surface if not us? You could grasp any one, for they are all ultimately from the realm of spirit. If the leaf is not to your liking reach again and take another, but take it first and then decide. When you meditate, reach and pluck the fruit we send to you and bite it, taste it. If you do not like it discard it and pluck again; if you do, then eat your fill.

✡

Cast your mind back to that time when you first became aware of your life and the place where you lived, the great city. You were filled with an essence; you were filled with questions about where you came from and why. As you enter as a child into the physical world this is what the soul demands to know. But the same questions are asked by the personality of the spiritual world once there is an awakening. Am I nothing? Will I just be left to die and rot while this exalted soul moves on? I who must suffer, who must trudge so wearily through this life, is this the thanks I will get? But the point of awareness that is 'I' belongs to God. In truth it is only on loan to the body for the duration of life. At the time of passing it is the tired, sick flesh that dies.

Not everyone can make the connection to spirit whilst in the body, in life. Many do not; they are content to see death as an end and the 'I' as a product of survival. Some have a facility to do both, to bring the light of soul into the darkness of the body, burdened by responsibility and toil. And then what happens to this burden, my son? It is exalted, it becomes the golden crown of experience, a lantern of hope for all who are in the darkness of despair.

✡

There comes a time in the course of spiritual development when that which is to be is glimpsed on the horizon. You look and wonder: 'Is that the dawn that I have been waiting for so long or is it a trick of the light? I have been so long in the darkness that I had almost given up hope, is my mind playing tricks? Is the depth of my longing causing me to imagine this? So many times I have been disappointed before, can this truly be that which I have secretly craved in my heart of hearts for all these long years?'

My brother, it is I, Yeshua, who speaks with you, not a trick of your mind. I stand before you now with Josephes. We too have been waiting for this moment. We have been with you all along like two who lead one who is blindfolded; who knows not whose arms he clings to, only that the arms are there as he stumbles forward. He hopes that they are those of his loved ones in spirit, and yet he dares not hope too much lest he be disappointed. Now, as you take the blindfold from your eyes you can see clearly who your companions are: you can take your place with us.

✡

The first day of a long awaited holiday in Spain. It is early morning, I am sitting on a bed in the spare room of the apartment we have borrowed in contemplation, the shutters are drawn and it is still cool. I am considering how I will use the holiday to meditate and reconnect to spirit. I have been very involved in preparing other publications for printing. I am afraid I have not meditated for over a month or more, but Malachi has other plans.

Recognise your holiday for what it is. It is no more than it appears to be, there is no hidden meaning and no hidden depth to that which you present before us at this time. You do not need to sit crosslegged, knuckles white, straining for a contact with spirit during your holiday. When you are relaxed you have no need of effort; spirit is in you and all around you. That posture which many take up, of sitting with teeth gritted intent upon a connection with God, is very largely a perceived antidote to the stress they feel in their lives.

It is a shame that the human creature is forced to live under conditions that produce this stress, for when humanity is liberated from the responsibilities that modern life brings he can be as naturally spiritual, as naturally in touch as any other of God's creatures. Enjoy your holiday my son. We walk beside you, we take pleasure in your delight, You do not need to talk to us in this way: we will talk to you in yours.

✡

There is an energy centre within the frame of man. It is positioned behind the heart chakra. This centre is the one towards which we come in order to speak with you. We say this because we realise that when you are involved in meditative practices, as now, there is always an anxiety that you will lose the link. You fear that neglecting the practice – as you were forced to do during the period of intense work before you went on holiday, and at our advice when you were on holiday – will cause the link to break or atrophy. The link cannot be lost. It is a mutual thing; we approach you as you send out a signal that you wish to speak with us. This approach is a matter as much of our volition as yours. If we were to leave it would be because our work with you was complete; but this is not the case and will not be the case for many years to come. There are many, many things that we will share with you and that others with whom we are in contact will share with you through us. But we are that voice which you know and recognise, that will bring the message from those different quarters.

✡

Enter, go into that altered state of consciousness that enables me to speak. My own preference is to make you aware of what I have to say in this manner, speaking in your heart at the time of meditation. It is different when I wish to communicate through you; then a little inspiration while you are talking is better. When I, Malachi, wish to speak to you personally, meditation is better. At other times it can be different, we can infiltrate your thoughts, we can work through unconscious suggestion whilst you are engaged in other activities. But this is our formal time for communication.

Each time we speak we generate energy; we increase infinitesimally the size of the portal through which we are able to approach. It is a different portal from that which Josephes uses. These portals are to do with your expectations of us. Each time we speak you become more aware of who we are, of our capabilities, of the kind of things that we may say in any given situation, and thus you build an expectation. When there is no expectation it is very easy to dismiss what comes; when there is too much expectation, that which comes may be dismissed because it does not fit. There must be some expectation, some anticipation of being met, of being spoken to, some recognition of the energy, of the lifestyle of he who speaks with you, otherwise communication cannot take place. This is why we share with you the scenes from our life, the things we did, so you will recognise the imagery of our coming.

✡

Among the hours that you spend at your computer you will find occasions when you look in vain for items that you cannot find. Then on another day or at another time when you are not looking for them, you find them easily. It is in the nature of consciousness to focus and in so doing, to exclude. It is like the lens of a camera brought into focus on one subject but leaving everything in the foreground and distance out of focus. When you are looking for something the focusing of consciousness can often exclude the very thing that you are searching for.

When you are communicating with us you must bring your thoughts to a pinnacle: not a pinnacle of focus in the sense of a point, but more a pinnacle of focused receptivity, of being open to whatever comes. Just before we started talking you saw before your eyes an orange light, did you not? You dismissed this, partly because of your dislike of this colour. But if we were to say that this light is the harbinger of our presence, then you would dismiss the signpost that leads the way to us.

Open-mindedness is such a difficult state to achieve: many of the judgments and censures that operate are not even within conscious control. You are trained to make judgments from a very early age; it is by making judgments that you find your way forward in the world, that you survive. 'This I will accept, this I will not. This I will believe in, this I will not. This kind of chair I like, this kind of chair, I do not.' Your entire identity is cohered around judgments. This is part of the problem with those who have Spiritual Teachers, especially those who are channelled. 'I agree when my Teacher says this, I do not like it when my Teacher says that.' And then, 'Because I do not like it, it cannot be something that my beloved Teacher would say. It must have come from the personality of the channel; I cannot believe that he would say such a thing.' This is how you create God in your own image is it not? But of course it is him. Spiritual Teachers are not just nice old beings who only ever say what you want to hear and make you feel good. Sometimes they have to be firm or contrary or distant, in order to set their loved ones on a new path.

So to be open-minded, accept what comes. We are not saying that you should accept all without any discrimination. This, too, we see going on – people standing up and claiming they have channelled this one and that one, when it is more a case of them wishing they had and they clearly have not. But you have to open up enough to make an informed judgment about what it is you are hearing. Do not dismiss it at the outset: dismiss it only when you have tried it on for size and found that it does not fit. Then make your judgment. 'Who is it who speaks? Is their advice to my liking? Does it feel right? Does it have the ring of truth?'

✡

Extrapolate from the theme that we have been sharing with you over the last year, and you will see a pattern in that which we have discussed you. Now you must ask yourself whether you are satisfied with this kind of contact. There is a reality to the kind of inspirational work that you are engaging in with us, and it is that you are conscious, you are awake. You still your thoughts and open your mind to us. We then project towards your mind certain energies which you convert, shall we say, to words and images which you speak into your tape recorder and then write down.

Now we are not projecting towards an empty vessel, we are not projecting towards a machine. We are projecting our energies towards a human being, a human being with a life history, with values, cares and fears. So, because of the method that we are using, your ability to interpret what we give is affected by the degree of open-mindedness that you are able to maintain. It would be very difficult for you to interpret from what we give something which you radically disagreed with or which threatened you personally, for example. This sometimes makes you look at what you have written and think, 'But I knew that, there is nothing new to me in this.' This is because fundamentally it is difficult for you to accept in the inspiration anything that does not have an assent within you.

Now this can be overcome to some extent with experience. On the other hand it is one of the limitations of the form of contact that we have with you. Not everything is perfect, my son, so do endeavour to keep an open mind during these times of meditation. Learn to expect the unexpected, explore the areas in your self that you are less familiar with, less comfortable with. It all serves to increase the field onto which we can project, and the acceptance of these things will enable you to expand the breadth of what you are able to receive.

✡

Still your mind, empty it of thought, offer us a fresh sheet of paper on which to write. Of course, we know that it is not blank; there is a difference between blankness and stillness. When you are still the paper appears blank, but in reality it is filled with words, ideas and images. They are just beneath the surface and can be awakened by our energy, cohered into new shapes, new meanings. We scan across them and place this thought with that idea and select an image from over there, and suddenly you see things differently. This image is as near to describing the perfect state of how we wish to work with you as we can achieve. You cannot build without materials; but if the owner of those materials has all manner of preconceived ideas about how they should be used, how they should fit together, and will not let go so that the builder can bring his influence and experience to bear, then all that can be built is that which already has been. In the case of inspiration the building materials are your knowledge your life, your ideas.

You can enter into the past in meditation and reap the experience stored there, but the past cannot be changed; all that can be changed about what has been written is your attitude to it. You can visit the future, but the future you will visit is but a possibility, or a probability; it has not yet been written, so it can be changed in any way that you wish. You can deepen the present in meditation: you can sit quietly and open to the time-lessness of your being, to the many levels of who you are. Or you can reach out with your mind to the spheres and realms that are beyond you. You can reach out to the great Teachers, to God, to anybody you wish. You have only to still the mind, to ask or visualise where you wish to go, and then to trust that which comes forward. There is no trick, no secret to medita-tion; it is primarily a matter of trust, imagination and open-mindedness. You can communicate with anything or anybody in your mind because your mind is exactly the same mind that is shared by all creation.

✡

After three days of quite strong contact with Malachi I have sat here for the last three days with no contact at all. It often seems to happen this way and I rather blame myself for it; I think it must be something I am doing wrong ...

Now this is very interesting. We realise that we have previously said that your mind should be like a blank sheet of paper, and so it should, but it also needs something on it that gives us a start, a grip. If you think about the process of crystallisation ... Think back to the crystals you used to grow as a child in a vessel filled with a saturated solution. To start the process off you would need to introduce a seed, something for the crystals to form around. You would drop in a seed crystal or some hard object, and around this the crystals would begin to form and grow. Now your mind is the vessel, we are akin to that saturated liquid and your question, or need, is the hard seed crystal around which the process of embellishment, of crystallisation takes place.

Now you may say, 'But there is not always a hard object in crystallisation.' And there always is – microscopic, you may not be able to see it with the naked eye, but it is there. Likewise in meditation, sometimes that seed is unconscious even to you. Then there are occasions when you sit in meditation and you are almost too passive. You empty your mind and wait quietly: we move around your aura, your mind, looking for something to which we can attach our thoughts, yet nothing really presents itself and then we must withdraw. So you could say that the failure on these occasions is twofold: there is our failure to find something significant to latch onto and embellish and your failure to present something significant to us.

We are both competing to be the receptive one, shall we say, and unless we have something positive we wish to say to you, we cannot play the masculine to your feminine. It is an interesting situation; but inspiration requires both the receptive and the positive principle to work. When both are aligned either way the process is seeded and then we can change poles: you can become the hard to our soft, and then it will turn and we become hard to your soft, and so forth, like a dance.

✡

It is not enough for you to want us to come and speak to you; there has to be some purpose in the communication. Perhaps this needs some clarification. We are not saying that desiring our company does not have a purpose, sometimes it does, but this is not necessarily always the case. We come with purpose;

we cannot give that which it does not suit our purpose to give. We have no choice in this matter, it is the law. The other thing that is worth recognising – how can we put this – we are not a dog that comes to a whistle, and by this we mean no offense to dogs. (In fact this is an illustration of some of our earlier discussions; the image of the dog is yours, from your life, and the meaning it is imbued with in this context is ours.) We come when your need fits with the matrix of our calling. It is a rather difficult combination of factors to explain in language, but the image of a key may help. Not all keys fit all locks and not all locks are opened by the same key; there has to be this match between lock and key. This is how we experience it: a meshing, a fitting of your need and ours. This enables contact, communication, but it is not always the case that there is a fit. It is not a failing; it is simply that the conditions in that particular moment are not those that facilitate contact.

As we have said many times before, one of the difficulties for those of us in spirit is that when we give advice or information we have to work within the parameters of what you find acceptable. There are certain ideas that you are open to and others that you are not. This opening and closing is virtually unconscious; we may approach in a particular way and you simply will not recognise us or what we offer. So for the kind of inspired work that we do with you we have to work with that which you already find acceptable and then extend or embellish the proposition, so to speak. Once we have established a dialogue we can expand upon the subject a little. Truly it is a matter of the imagination, the ability to imagine. If you can allow this free rein it gives us a ballroom to dance in, but if you have only a relatively small area of possibility that is acceptable to you then we must, of course, content ourselves with dancing in the broom cupboard.

I often start my meditation with a prayer. The one I most often use is, 'May the God within me bring me that which I need.' This morning Malachi picks up on it.

And may the God within you bring you peace. Cast out your preconceptions, cast out your anticipations, cast out your hopes and fears. For the time being forget what we have said about asking questions; for the moment just be still, be still. Then what will come to you will be that which is true. Talk into your tape recorder. Those words that form in the stillness, you do not have to make sense of them; they will make sense of themselves. Within no more than one week you will experience a shift. We realise that your meditation has not been easy and we appreciate that you have stuck with it. It is not easy to come into your room and receive nothing, and then to come back to sit again and receive nothing a second time and a third and a fourth. Even those with the best of intentions would get disheartened, would begin to dread sitting down to another failure. What can we say? If we had a wand we would gladly wave it – but great profit comes from great endeavour.

Just let me speak; it matters not what those first words are. They break the silence, that is all, and once the silence is broken the channel is opened and I can fill the space. Remember, expectations are the curse of those who do the kind of inspired meditations that you do. Expectations are an astringent. They close the pores to the process of spiritual osmosis.

Changes and problems

This is a rather difficult chapter. So far you may have got the impression that my contact with spirit has, on the whole, been very positive and smooth, but the reality has been far from this. The problems have not been with Malachi but with myself, my ambivalence and my resentment at the changes that this path has demanded. At times I have found myself being quite ungracious about what I have been offered, but if this book is to be an accurate representation of the process then this chapter deserves a place.

What does it mean to teach? To impart information. To impart experience. To bring forward the innate wisdom of the student in a particular path or direction.

Some of what is occurring in your life at this time has its roots in this last statement. When a Teacher such as I, Malachi, establishes himself in the aura of their chosen pupil there can ensue something of a struggle. The soul listens to the wisdom of the Teacher, and responds to the teachings and to the path that is opened before it by the Teacher. The personality is then entreated to follow, to change direction, to let certain things go and to embrace other, new things. This is what is happening in your case. But the self does not let go easily; why should it? It seeks to maintain what it has always known, and then the confrontation between the will of the self and the will of the soul is experienced.

There is a saying: better the devil you know ... But this is a case of a new alignment being necessary for your growth and development. This involves a shift in emphasis, a shift in values, a change of direction.

Follow me, my son ...

✡

I really don't know how to blend what I am learning with you with my counselling a work.

Think about the blind man, who has known sight and then in mid life is struck down with an illness that causes him to lose his ability to see. He must then find his way by developing his other senses: hearing, smell, touch and intuition. Those who have developed a skill are a little like this man and this man is a little like you; when one sense is highly developed and serves you well, it is easy to ignore the others. But we wish you to open to the others; when one sense or ability is very developed, so are the expectations and judgments that go with it. It is in the less developed senses that there is more opportunity for perceiving spirit. These senses are innocent; like children, they do not question, they accept what is presented to them.

The predominant colour in your aura is deep rose pink, a colour that many within the helping professions share. Recently gold was added and now you cannot expect things to remain the same; there will be changes, there is change already. The gold brings the impact of the purely spiritual to the depth of human understanding represented by the pink. It can be a very powerful combination, but you must be prepared to allow the gold to augment and uplift the pink. At the current time you tend to use the pink to block out the gold. This is not particularly surprising; the pink is what you are used to, the gold appears as a stranger to you and those things that are strange are not so easily accepted.

Sit quietly and relax. Visualise yourself surrounded in pink, your deep rose pink, and then gently become aware of the gold suffusing the edges, and slowly pouring into the pink, rolling and disturbing its depth until bright flashes of gold disrupt its surface and send shafts of golden light through its depths. Then slowly let it settle and feel the peace it brings. Feel what the gold brings to the pink and the pink brings to the gold; let them interact and grow together. Do this each morning.

✡

The following morning, after I have completed the meditation as prescribed by Malachi:

A nd what is your feeling?

It is hard to describe ... it is depth and peace, not deep peace but depth and peace ... or perhaps peaceful depth.

In much of your daily life you spend hours listening, interpreting, working with the unconscious. You enter the darkness that your clients bring in order to help them understand themselves and their path better. When you enter this darkness, the depth surrounding the human soul with your clients, you need a light to guide you. All who are involved in your profession need this; without it you would become lost, unable to distinguish the territory, or what belongs to you and what belongs to them. Thus far you have used the light of reason, augmented by your intuition as your guide. But the gold can bring a different light to bear, and it has the additional benefit of bringing this peace, this healing to your work. If you trust the gold light, invite it in consciously, you will be doing a great deal to cooperate with the changes and transitions that you, and those you speak with, are involved in.

I often feel isolated in both the communities I belong to, the spiritual and the psychological. People who are involved in spiritual work rather turn their noses up at psychological perspectives, or at any rate seem fearful of them. On the other hand, some of my psychological colleagues dismiss the spiritual as ungrounded, escapist and an avoidance. Yet when I share some of the simple perspectives I have learned through meditation in the training groups I work with, the participants are usually very positive, they want more. But professionally neither side seems to want to take the other too seriously, although in my view they are the perfect complements.

The spiritual people seem to think that understanding the teaching is enough, that it never needs to be actually translated into behaviour. But practical psychology has an excellent framework for helping people understand and express themselves and to relate to others. Take defences for example: many of my spiritual friends are extremely defensive about their pain, not surprisingly. But in my psychological work I have found that when pain or longing is acknowledged, spoken about truthfully rather than denied, on many occasions something quite beautiful happens. The very thing that was defended against transforms into a very pure form of love, a very deep compassion for humanness, and a consequent understanding of humanity: it is a healing. As if, when difficulties are openly acknowledged and the simple truth is spoken with a pure heart, the hand of Christ himself reaches down and releases the individual. And because this love springs from an inner fountain it is theirs to keep, unlike words in a book or even the words of a Teacher. It is the alchemy of the heart.

In my practice and in the groups I teach and work with this happens all the time. I dare say that it is close to the lived experience of the soul, but within my spiritual community I find often that the defenses are so brittle, people seem to be so averse to this notion of speaking the simple truth, that the process of transformation never gets beyond first base. Perhaps I expect too much of the spiritual types. I have to admit that I expect far more from them than I do from my clients. Perhaps my assumption that there even is a simple truth is arrogant; perhaps my spiritual community is not the place for this kind of thing anyway. All this I am prepared to accept, but I will not let go of this potential for transformation, or of the precursive honesty that is required from individuals to enable it.

Through the pink to the gold. Does this describe what you are talking about? It takes great courage to walk the path that you are talking about, great courage to overcome the fear that once again, when exposed, the delicate feelings and longings of the soul will be ridiculed, ignored or criticised. It is also a capacity that not all have; they have other capacities but not this one. We always advocate the more gentle path ...

Yes, in common with many other spiritual traditions, 'think positively, ignore the difficulty, turn away from the shadow, don't feed it and it will go away.' But I don't agree. Ignore the shadow and it runs your life, ignore the difficulties and problems and you miss the healing and integration of its qualities when the shadow is confronted, accepted and embraced in the heart.

You are strong, strong in your opinion and strong in your focus and dedication to what you have chosen. But this strength ... it can be a failing as well as a quality, can it not? You do have a little of Elijah in you; it can frighten people. They do not see the gentleness that drives your approach. They do not see how much you hope for their healing, and they do not always see the sincerity of your heart. It is a problem, is it not? Perhaps sometimes they feel pushed into a corner. There is more than one way to skin a cat, my son. Let us respond to your dilemma in this way: stop now and meditate awhile, see the gold and the pink together as we described earlier.

Very well. [I meditate for a few minutes]

And what did you see?

I saw billowing clouds of rose pink, then a soft gold suffusing the the pink. After that the pink started to slowly roll and boil, and what seemed like hundreds of small golden mirrors sent beams of golden light piercing and flashing through the pink and out in to the room around me.

And then?

Then I felt something very beautiful, very soft and gentle, a great peaceful presence.

The Christos comes with the gold and is there for all. No longer will that hand reach down towards you, my son. If you let it, it will reach out from your own heart.

I woke up this morning with my head spinning. My inability to integrate my spiritual perspectives with those of psychology is starting to drive me mad. A five-year training with a large institution, followed by twenty years of sitting down in front of people every day, supervision, trying to maintain professional standards ... I am full of things I have learned that have in turn become virtually unconscious assumptions about the nature of relationship and healing. I think that it would be a great deal easier for me now if I had never turned counselling into a profession; maybe I would be more open to change.

Every success ultimately becomes a limitation, does it not? Consider primitive man, unable to use anything but the most rudimentary of tools to help him in his quest for food and clothing. Then one day some creative member of the tribe is inspired to pick up a sharp flint and use it for cutting, a revolution that changes the lifestyle of the whole tribe. Others come and shape these flints for different purposes – arrowheads for hunting, scrapers and knives. They feel that they are advancing, they feel that compared to their past they are lucky, blessed, and indeed they are. But then one day a member of another tribe approaches, is welcomed, and he has a bronze axe for trade.

The flint knives were not bad, they were not wrong, they

served the needs of the tribe well; but who would insist on continuing to use flint when there is such a wonderful material as bronze available? Progress always casts a shadow behind itself. But it does not have to. The wiser of the tribal elders would give thanks for the flint and would give the man who recognised its worth an honoured place in the history of the tribe, rather than cursing him because he did not discover bronze in the first place.

Flint is hard but difficult to work; bronze is soft but very flexible in its uses. Each has its own place within the scheme of things. Progress is always a matter of steps. You cannot be at the goal unless you are prepared to walk to it one step at a time, and all must walk; there are no magical solutions. So it is with your work: one step at a time, and take care not to curse the pink for not being gold.

✡

One thing I haven't found easy about this path is the fear of loss of freedom, of my autonomy. Not that it has been taken from me, but I do tend to prioritise all those things that pertain to my purpose and ignore others. I am sure that this is a character trait as much as anything else – I am a bit of an 'all or nothing' person – but still, I no longer feel I have the options or freedoms that I used to enjoy. Malachi picks up on this when I start a new section of my writing after a New Year celebration.

The first day of a new year, the first page of the rest of your life. There is that which has been written and that which has yet to be; the future pages are blank, empty pages upon which you can write whatever you wish. But we know that these pages are not entirely blank. They have, shall we say, the imprint of the Masters already upon them, for you have given yourself to us and we have prepared the way for you. You are free, but where your work is concerned you have sold your soul. And what do we hear you say – that you did not get a very good price for it? Like all good investments the return at the beginning is poor; it is only later, when the work has been put in, that you reap the rewards. Doing business with spirit is no different from doing business elsewhere, the dividends are related to the investment. And what, you ask, is the return on your investment? We will pay you with fulfilment; we will satisfy your deepest longings; we will lead you to the doorway of bliss, we will bring you peace and erase fear from your life.

When the businessman surveys his empire, when the mountaineer gazes out from the mountaintop, when the runner feels the tape across her chest, they all glimpse a momentary satisfaction. And what is this satisfaction, that these men and women will devote their lives to achieve, will make almost any sacrifice for? It is an echo of a deeper truth, a truth that is the birthright of all humanity. In that moment of triumph they remember, however fleetingly, their birthright. Believe us when we say that some members of humanity sell their souls for far, far less than you have. Would you rather have the original, the work of the Creator Himself, or would you sooner settle for the copy? We think not. You act humbly, and so you should. You say that you do not know what the future holds, and perhaps you do not. You wonder, why me? But if you look deep into your heart we are sure that you do know one thing, and that is that like so may others at this time, you have been called and found fit. You are chosen and you have chosen; you have made a pact with God.

✡

I had a nasty accusatory row with my wife last night; what I said was neither fair nor justified. I am teaching this weekend, just now it's 6.45 in the morning and I don't want to go. The events of the last few weeks, the usual January budget problems, getting back into work after the holidays. I have been pushing myself quite hard; possibly this is why my meditations have been so unsatisfactory. I am not really in the flow, so to speak. Clients arrive and I just want them to go; they appear to me more as chores than people. Now I will be spending my weekend working; this week and next we have guests staying. I know this space: when I am under pressure I start to feel burdened and then, hardly knowing I'm doing it, I start to force myself through.

My son, it is within your capacity to do all these things and more. It is within the mind that the problem becomes unmanageable – the mind that is driven by the feelings, which are driven by past experience of poverty. You take things upon yourself. This is a quality that we cherish in you; it means that you can be relied upon not to cast the blame elsewhere when things get difficult, nor to wait for others to relieve the situation, but to do what you can with what you have. Although you recognise the futility of pointing the finger at others, we are aware that you are not above pointing it at yourself, and when you do you close down. You prepare for battle and the armour that protects you from pressure also protects you from our assistance. We stand back helpless, despairing, watching as you unsuccessfully try to cope alone. In truth the outer pressures that you face at this time are little compared with the inner pressures. We cannot force ourselves upon you; we have to wait until we are invited. You are not alone but you must reach out a hand and take what is offered. Truly you can walk alone or we can carry you, but is it not best that we walk together?

✡

I was thinking about my inspired writing in the bath before this meditation; I worry about it constantly at the moment. Is it is truly inspired by Malachi or is it all just a fancy, a regurgitation of my own hotchpotch of New Age understandings?

Proceed cautiously towards your goal, make no claims; just allow your words to speak for themselves. There will come a time when doubts will not weigh so heavily on your mind. Utter conviction is not something that we would recommend in any case; it leads to arrogance. Doubts have their place within the scheme of things; they are not there for no reason.

✡

I have been absent from my meditations for some months. It has been a very difficult time. Despite encouragement from many sources I have been very critical of my writing, very doubtful about whether Malachi even exists beyond my own imagination. I have not exactly felt suicidal, but I have not wanted to live very much either. As time passed I became less and less inclined to pick up my tape recorder or even to meditate. The less I meditated and wrote, the more I lost my zest for life. I became depressed, started to drink heavily and began to lose interest in everything. What was most alarming about this whole process was that I just didn't care that it was happening. Finally one day I did meditate, and the following words came through, followed by very poignant imagery. The imagery was pervaded with a feeling of very deep understanding and acceptance. The whole episode taught me an important lesson.

Daily meditation is not an absolute requirement, we ask only that you return to it. We are aware of you whether you meditate or not, but what becomes more difficult if you do not is your awareness of us.

I can see an image of several men squatting on the ground looking through something that is between them, a fire I think. They are dressed in deerskin; they are North American Indians, and they are involved in some deliberations. One stands up and comes towards me; he nods gravely and introduces himself. I know him well; he is a Hopi called Little Cloud who was a spirit guide of mine for about eight years. He appears now as an old man.

He takes me gently by the hand and leads me back to the group of men around the fire. I squat with them and look into the white ash, where there are one or two faintly glowing embers. Little Cloud says that I have been brought here to be with this group because there is something they understand about me that my other Spiritual Teachers find difficult to appreciate.

He says that they understand my longing for the earth, for the peace of death. He says that my doubts about my writing have energised this longing, that my soul purpose is to write and if I turn my back on this I am turning my back on all that gives my life its meaning, its purpose. If there is no point to life I may as well return to the great round, and my soul is beginning to prepare for this. The others are nodding, as if they understand too. He says that they understand how hard it can be for me to continue sometimes. They understand that portion of my soul that would rather be with Wakuntanka, the Great Spirit. They say there is no shame in this but for the time being I must stay because I have a task to fulfil.

Their words release a flood of tears.

✡

The next day another Teacher came into my meditations, also known to me – an Atlantean called Adolphus, a crystal Master.

I bring my greetings to you this day, and I bring to you word from the Masters who seek to bring you only upliftment.

Come, and in your mind walk with me to a place of healing, a place of peace. Those beautiful healing caves, those healing pools at the time of Atlantis, destroyed now by time, still exist in the spirit realms. There are attendants who understand the needs of those who come. Follow me.

I can see a pool of either pale smoky quartz or citrine. The bottom is a vast, smooth slab of crystal; it must be one face of an enormous stone buried in the ground. It is surrounded by large crystal points and stones; a path leads down between them into the water. The water is not very deep, maybe two feet or less, and it is warm. I can sit in it and lie back. The water has the most extraordinary quality, very soft. There are people around who are responsible for the pool and they are softly chanting a specific word. This seems to be the word that energises the crystals and starts the healing, I could stay here all day, but I have clients coming so perhaps, if I can, I will leave my soul here and get on with my work.

✡

It's starting to sound as though I do nothing but complain, but in fact this entry is separated from the previous ones by about six months! It came during another bout of self-doubt.

Everlasting is the nature of soul. It always has been and will always be of God, and God remains a mystery even to us. It is said that at the point when the understanding of God is attained it is no longer possible to communicate it save through the means that God uses: the act of creation itself ...

How come you never tell me anything that I don't already know?

Does the apprentice not learn by copying the works of the master? You are still in development, my son, and anyway, have you not realised by now that we are of one mind? We do not just speak when you sit and meditate. We influence your thoughts constantly. An idea that you had yesterday, remembering a particular passage or verse you read years ago – are you so certain that it is not spirit that propagates these seeds? If we were to communicate only when you are sitting still and meditating you could never learn what you will need in order to face the challenges of the future.

Each one within his or her own sphere of influence will take up the demands of the next decade or so. This will require great forbearance and great forbearance requires slow training. Once these events are accepted and the methods of dealing with them are established they need not cause terrible hardship, but they will need wisdom, wisdom and understanding, and these cannot be built overnight; it takes time and constant repetition. So if you are impatient with us, we apologise. We also remind you that we are still the masters and you are still the pupil; loved greatly, but still the pupil.

✡

Sometimes I think that what I write quite moving and yet the next day I read it again, putting myself in the position of a potential reader, and it seems that no one will believe it. It leads me to doubt the source.

We would put this differently. In your heart we feel that you know exactly what the source of your writing is. It is nothing short of what you claim it to be. But your thinking, influenced by the beliefs of the time, argues with this constantly. This is partly because you don't want to be disparaged and ridiculed, so you play it down. If you had made it up yourself rather than it coming from a dialogue with a greater part of yourself, perhaps you feel that it would be more acceptable, more in tune with the expectations of the times and thus less open to scepticism.

All creativity comes from a dialogue with something greater, as artists down the ages will attest. Perhaps your reticence is because that something greater in your case has a name – Josephes or Malachi. Really, what does it matter? It all comes from the great pool of wisdom and knowledge that is in the non-physical realm. Call it mind, call it spirit, call it what you like, it won't change the fact of its existence. Some are lucky enough to have that knowledge mediated through a particular spiritual personality; others connect to it in a more general way.

Electricity is a good example. It is not confined to the wiring of your house: domestic electricity is simply energy utilised in one specific way. Such energy is transformed into movement or light for your convenience and entertainment, but first it is just energy, and after it is discharged through your appliances and screens it returns to the great reservoir of energy whence it came. This reservoir is what you would call latent or potential energy and it is truly vast. Another way of describing it would be as free energy, energy that has not yet been put to the yoke.

There are certain movements, rites or scientific procedures that can transform the energy within this great store into those recognisable and utilisable forms of energy that power your needs. These rites are common and understood: the coils on an armature, the movement of traffic, even the barking of your dog. When a scientist or engineer initiates the process of nuclear fission he is releasing energy from this store. When an animal drops its head to graze in a pasture it is releasing this energy. When a human being raises a hammer to beat steel into a tool this energy is utilised and released.

It is the same with healing, with meditation, with your inspired writing: there is a vast store of energy that is available on demand. When groups gather together for earth healing, for example, a massive amount of this is released and grounded into the planet. When you sit and meditate as you are now doing, you switch on the lights, then you raise the hammer in a different way. It is not so difficult to do, but the dominance of the scientific principle in this age has led all people to some extent to believe that this energy can only be released through scientific procedures. If it is not, then they question; they demand replicable results and above all, physical evidence. If we were to say, for example, that the ancients could levitate things through chanting, or that they could heal with a touch or with crystals would you believe it?

They could, you know. It is like when you are working with a client who has been victimised by a parent and who considers that they have been wronged unfairly; it is always a shock when they realise how like that parent they behave in their own relationships. It is the same with those who meditate, who connect to the voice of a Spiritual Teacher; each one says, 'Well I get this information, but really I don't know whether to believe it or not.' Each one craves evidence; each one applies the scepticism and principles of the physical sciences to their endeavours. If we were able to drop an inscribed stone tablet in your lap while you are at your meditations we would; but we cannot, and until we are able to you will have to accept those pictures and words that we do place before you.

✡

There are squabbles breaking out in the spiritual community I belong to, and I am thinking about unity.

When we speak of unity we mean unity of purpose. What we do not mean is sameness. Within unity of purpose there is room enough for an infinite diversity of approach. We do not ask that those of you who band together to do some spiritual work think in the same way. We do not ask that you behave in the same way, or that you feel the same things as one another. We ask only that you learn to appreciate the differences and tolerate the shortcomings of one another.

We do not ask that you blindly condone the behaviour of one another; there is always room for improvement. Rather, we ask that you discuss your differences with each other in a rational way. It is the very differences of approach and thinking that are creative, that refine understanding, that lend depth and authenticity to your work. Nor do we ask you to blindly accept what we say, but that you search your hearts for the resonance that is there. When we talk of unity we ask that each one of you bear in mind the teachings, the purpose and the love that is at the heart of the work, within the hearts of those who participate in it, and prioritise these.

✡

Things are getting very tight in our home financially, with the two adults self-employed, one son working for a low wage and the other starting art college.

We would entreat you thus. Take to yourself those things that you need and set aside those things that you do not; in this way you will always have abundance. Letting go of the old, moving on to the new, this is the way of abundance. Abundance and accumulation for its own sake are incompatible; accumulation of this sort is a kind of pride, it is trying to be the provider as well as he who is provided for. To live in true abundance requires a kind of humility, an acceptance of what life offers, rather than an attempt to dominate life to ensure that it offers exactly what you feel you want.

✡

Extrapolate from your situation. You fear that it is all being taken away, that you will have nothing left. But think of the laws of balance: where there is reduction in one department there is increase in another; it cannot be otherwise. As your income reduces, the time you have to spend on other things increases. You have only to trust, to draw on that great pool of energy and to allow yourself to receive.

Within every difficulty there is an opportunity. If it were not so everyone would be defeated by the difficulties they encounter. Built into each problem that life presents are the steps that enable you to go beyond it, to listen to that problem and to respond to it from the point of view of your own growth. When I walked the earth there were the famine years; then hopes, plans and expectations had to be shelved and energies focused on survival.

Then afterwards there was always something that had been learned from that privation – a new way of managing our resources, and a deeper understanding of the needs and foibles of those who relied on those resources.

✡

Although there have not really been any material improvements I am starting to feel a little more positive about my future.

Examine the events that now surround you. Nothing has really changed since last we talked; what has changed are your feelings about things. The effect of attitudes on perception is true of many; it takes very little to trigger fear in the hearts of humanity, and fear begets fear. It is like a beacon that attracts to itself the evidence it needs to prove its assertions for the future. But just as fear can grow from a speck of doubt, so it can be dispelled by a speck of hope. Consider how much time is spent working, planning, in order to build a bulwark against catastrophe, and how little time is spent in hoping, in trusting, in asking what the true meaning of events are. You have nothing to fear; give yourself into God's hands and trust.

✡

With all the changes that are currently occurring in my life I wish you could give me some clues as to what the future holds for me, some certainty that I could rely on.

It is not for us to reveal it, except in its most general sense, and we would not recommend any medium who claims to be able to do so. Those that do are generally just holding up a mirror to the wishes of those that seek them out; they are the psychics, able to read the aura of those that come to them. The Teachers who speak through true spiritual mediums work within sacred law, and the law states that the free will of the individual is paramount. So your future is what you make it; it is built of your visions, your hopes and your choices.

There are auspicious times, times when we can see that the currents are moving in a particular direction – perhaps one that suits a direction that you are also going in – and these we can reveal. In this way we can see when opportunities might arise, but the detail, the names, dates, places and what you should do about them? No. This is a matter of free will and responsibility. So we can say no more than we have already said: your work is with the word, in thought, in speech and in writing.

✡

Sometimes I feel as if I could sit here for weeks at a time without making any contact whatsoever. It knocks my confidence, and makes it difficult for me to continue.

Well do not let it knock your confidence; nobody sits down and makes instant contact with spirit, it takes a lifetime of practice. Some of those in spirit come in response to the need of humanity. Some come to the need of the individual. Some come because of their own need. In your case we most often come because of your need, but that does not mean we have nothing to say to humanity. Are you not part of humanity? And in speaking to you, do we not speak to humanity?

✡

There are still some difficulties in the spiritual group that I belong to. Malachi's comment to the group is this:

There is so much that awaits you; you are standing at the doorway of a vast treasure house. Stored within it are gifts beyond your wildest imaginings. You have been told this and yet you are also told that you are not yet within it. So you search about, you ask yourselves: How do I enter? Where and what is the key, and why will my Spiritual Teachers not tell me? Why are they so enigmatic?

There is no key. The door opens light to the touch; those within are beckoning you forward and yet you huddle outside. This great door opens on the breeze of belief; you have only to see yourselves inside and so will it be. It is said that the way of a dog is that if he is hit with a stone he bites another dog. It could be said that you have been hit with a stone, the stone of enlightenment, but you are not dogs. So stop biting each other and step forward in majesty and grace, step forward into your birthright, into the treasure house. Then you can share it with others: those who come and, like you, stand at the door bewildered, disbelieving, not trusting. Show them that all that keeps them from the truth is themselves, their illusions. Show them that what they consider to be reality is in fact no more than a tiny part of a greater truth. Then show them that greater truth, the Kingdom of God.

✡

When you enter a spiritual group or commit deeply to a group of any kind it is no easy task, from seeing yourself as an individual, a whole body, a whole unit, to recognise that you are but an arm or a foot of a far greater body. But this is the truth. It is not easy to surrender individuality; to step into the void, as it were, is a terrible challenge. But believe us when we say that it is only a void when you look into it from the side on which you stand. From our side we see you standing squinting towards us, your eyes misty, unable to see clearly what you are stepping towards.

You hear our words calling you. You listen; they touch your heart. 'There must be something good there.' It is only when you have made the step that your eyes will be opened and yes, it is a sad irony that this is so, but it is so with a reason. We know what it is that you are stepping into and in your souls you know too, but left to their own devices your personalities would never step forward in a thousand years. You are blinded. Your eyes have been put out so that you will conquer your fears and allow your souls to take the lead.

✡

I see an image of two large, booted feet stamping down together on a small hill and that hill erupting into a miniature volcano. It is an image of suppression and subsequent eruption. Perhaps it means that I am suppressing, suppressing and resisting the changes I am faced with.

The imperative to change is stronger than you. Ultimately you will be unable to resist it.

I would say that I am not actively resisting change, rather that I am deeply ambivalent about it.

We would agree with this, but you want the changes on your terms; certain things you will allow and others you will not. For example you will accept the changes as long as they do not lead to too much disruption in your family life.

I have certain responsibilities and I don't want to be so reduced in circumstance that survival issues start to dominate my life and I have no time left for doing anything else.

On the other hand your survival can be paid for by your new activities.

Perhaps yes, in the long term, but I am concerned about now. Writing books is fun but it pays damn all! What a difficult time this is. I feel forced into change and I resent it deeply. Over the last three or four months clients have steadily left until my work is in ruins. I have no savings; I am having to face drastic action. What a terrible thing resistance is! A rage so deep that it spits in the face of God. And this is not a God who has forced Himself on me; it is the same God that I have prayed to, longed for and been nurtured by. Now He comes in his gentle chariot and I turn away from His love. To me He appears like a destroying angel, breaking up my routines, making space in my life so that he can find a home in it, and I slam the door in His face. 'How much will it cost?' asks the accountant. 'Will my family be fed? asks the father. 'Will the house have to go and will there be time for wine?' I ask, and 'What will people think of me?' And if God could speak he would say:

Those things are not your home, your home is with Me, and as you have longed for Me, so I long to find a home in you.

And such is the depth of my resentment that if I had a rusty knife in my hand right now I would cut His words to shreds and leave them hanging in tatters.

✡

And some mornings like today, when I have had yet another unsuccessful meditation, I take my bath and in the warmth and stillness I can feel my future massing and crawling at the back of my neck, filled with portent, demanding my attention. Like a sultry grey tide that will inevitably wash round any obstacles and submerge them. And I know that I am one of those obstacles. I am like a tiny pebble on the beach shouting at that great impassive sea to go back, go back.

    My heart is so faint, my body so weak I can hardly stand up, but my nails are strong and I will hang on, while there is strength left in my body to deny Him, I will.

✡

Then when my rage is spent there is a shift of sorts, perhaps a new beginning. At least now I am prepared to acknowledge that I have responsibility for my own difficulties rather than trying to punish God for them.

✡

This year, the year before the Millennium, is the final purification, the emptying of the vessel, when all false prophets must be cast out.

✡

I feel as if I have a sheet of ice on my skin. It consists of everything that anyone has ever said about who I am or what I am or why I am, in many cases none too kindly. 'Not very bright but good with his hands, too fat, too aggressive, selfish.' All those beliefs I have about myself, conscious and unconscious, that were never generated by my own heart, and prevent me from being who I am. Without them I feel naked, exposed, and with them I feel frozen. It is not any belief per se, but the sum of them all, that whole subtle, pervasive mechanism that psychologists call the superego, that is brought into focus at the moment.

✡

I have been asked to stand down from a teaching post. The news is not a total surprise but has come at a bad time, as I have a lot of status tied up in that work. I seem to be losing so much at the moment. Despite my assertion that I would hold on until death it is as if my fingers are being prized off all the things I use to bolster my identity in the world. I feel like shouting at God, 'What more do you want? Haven't I given enough yet?'

You have written one book from your own inspirations; another is already nearing completion. You have four, five, six more books in you, all inspired from your Higher Self. What will fill these books is a different strain of teaching, closely allied to that which Joseph of Arimathea gives but different, unique in its preparation, with its own particular twist, its own particular attitude. Truth is absolute; there is only one truth, but this truth is expressed in so many different ways, you need look no further than that which you have already received. It has been stated many times that your work is with the word – spoken, written, or thought – the word of your experience, the words given to you from your Higher Self. So let go those things which are going of their own account; then turn to receive the new that is coming towards you.

There is nothing that you are facing at this moment in time that cannot be overcome, but it cannot be overcome by re-establishing what has been ...

I am really sorry, this is making me absolutely furious! I just can't hear what you are saying, I feel preached at and patronised ...

Then it is because, in our concern, we are failing to find a language that you can accept during this most trying of times. We apologise and withdraw.

✡

I am drawn to the image of a huge limestone church we visited in Aubeterre in the Charente in France this summer, literally carved from the inside of a mountain. Inside there is a monument to Joseph of Arimathea. I can see Malachi and he is beckoning me to follow him through a tunnel in one corner. We have to bend somewhat to get through. After a while the tunnel opens into a vast temple of light. In complete contrast to the monolith we have just left, the objects and architecture here are made of light, golden, yellowy and pearlescent. Malachi beckons me to catch up and walk alongside him. We seem to have come in from the wings rather than the main entrance. He is saying to me that the stone church we left behind is a representation of this temple. He says that if you walk away from an ordinary church and you do not ask about the source of the inspiration that created it, then you have missed the point of the architecture and you have missed the point of the church. I look up and around at the temple we are in. The scale is epic; it has the feeling not so much of being a public place but of belonging to all. Malachi tells me that this is the temple of Christ and that he has brought me here because we stand on the threshold of the Second Coming, not in the form of a man but in the hearts of all humanity, the age of the risen Christ.

✡

New Year's Day, 2000.

Into the difficult waters that humankind is having to navigate at this time has been dropped a depth charge. Nothing has changed, still the tides conflict with the winds, the storms rage – and yet nothing is the same. Deep within the ocean there is now a great source of stillness and that stillness is filled with everything that is necessary to build a new world, a world that is yet closer, more attuned to the realm of spirit than any that man has managed before. The energy within that charge is inexhaustible, it will surface and continue to surface until it is no longer required.

It will emerge from within, not from some abstract source above, because now it is grounded in the fabric of the planet. As you sent your lights, your fireworks and your lasers up into the sky so we answered by sending the lights of spirit towards you. But we did not stop at the surface of the planet, we sent our light deep into the core, and within that light was the light of the Christos. And there it dwells, in the crystals and the soil of the planet, in the hearts and the sinews of humanity, as yet unrecognised by most, waiting to be used, waiting to be seen and touched and awakened by those like yourselves, who have the benefit of a little foreknowledge. And now we have taken up your time with our little eulogy, here is the voice of Yeshua, that you long to hear in your heart but never ask for:

> My brother, did you think I would let this moment pass without speaking with you myself? I offer you my hand; we all need a little help from time to time do we not? So place your arm in mine and we will walk together again as friends and companions, just as we did before.

✡

Now, as you are editing the first book of our words, this seems a good place to pause, to look back upon your progress so far. What we would like to review is how you have developed over the years, how you have built, step by step, a trust in the voice of spirit. Think back through your life to your teenage years when you were aware of night travels and night paralysis. We could say that these experiences were defining ones; you had irrefutable evidence that you existed beyond your body and then had to find a way to make sense of it. You were attracted to the martial arts and the religious philosophies which infused them. You read books on psychology, asking philosophical questions about the nature of existence, about who you truly were. You explored different avenues: Tarot, the I Ching, the Tibetan texts and the great oracles. Your painting helped you understand the language of symbols and intuition. Then came your training as a psychologist, learning how to access the unconscious, to work with images, symbols, the will and the primacy of the mind. Then you became involved in the beauty and elegance of the Native Indian spiritual tradition.

These were all ways of going beyond yourself to a more spiritual reality, but only gradually did you begin to truly understand that the spiritual dimension you sought was not outside yourself but within. Another defining moment was your meeting with the channel, and speaking with Joseph of Arimathea through that medium; it was a direct spiritual voice, but still through a medium. Then came a major turning point, your introduction to the gentlest of spirit guides, Little Cloud. You made a discipline of meditation, and began to write. For two years you wrote anything that came into your mind during meditation, then gradually you were able to discern within that writing the voice of Josephes, which you collated and published as a book. For four years he became your daily guide and companion, along with Adolphus and Llane to help you with your understanding of crystals. Now for nearly four years it has been myself who has guided you, and you are turning my words into a little book.

Take this moment to pause, to look back and see how gradual and painstaking the changes and developments have been. It is over fifteen years since you met the channel, ten years since you started writing yourself. You can see the progression: you didn't just suddenly wake up one day and start speaking to a spiritual master; in truth you have had to work for every gain. There was the awakening, the searching, synchronicity, people who came to help, people who came to hinder. En route to the spiritual there was a flirtation with the psychic, with the astral*, the struggles with inflation and unworthiness – all important stages. Your consciousness has had to move through the spheres, each step a preparation for the next, but steps to where? It would not be fair just to look back without a nod to the future, would it?

There will be more teachers who will come to you in time, teachers greater than I; but it is not the teacher who is important, it is the teachings. As time passes and you gain in confidence in this work you will find that what you will be able to channel will become more specific; you will find that you will be able to risk more concrete and practical statements, perhaps even quite controversial material. At the beginning it is always safer to stick to that which brings hope and upliftment and this will always be so, but we also wish to speak on the practical methods that people can use to gain liberation. So this is a little of what the future holds, and we trust that this small introductory volume will be the first of many.

✡

*The spheres or planes of consciousness that come before the causal plane.

Chapter 5

Spiritual inspiration and counselling

For the past twenty years I have worked as a counsellor and psychotherapist. Traditionally psychological and spiritual perspectives do not make good bedfellows. Much of the following chapter concerns an inner struggle, often played out externally, between my traditional work and the new, spiritual sources that were starting to inform my life. This generated some very real fears about my survival. Personally I do not believe that spirit is in the least bit opposed to survival; why should it be? But my poor old ego, which had been running the show fairly successfully, and had got me this far, now had to let go to something greater.

✡

I am concerned about how the way I work is changing; I feel somewhat out on a limb. I don't really know what I am doing any more. When there is a specific need for psychotherapy this is not a problem, but there are many people who come who are not clear what they need. With such as these, what I do cannot really be described as psychotherapy and yet it does appear to be effective.

M y son, you are growing out of the shell that has contained you, and this growth will not fit any of the forms that are currently available in the field of psychology. We feel that you already know that when somebody comes and sits with you, the verbal dialogue is not the only one: there is a dialogue of energy, a transmission, there is a dialogue of souls, of Higher Selves. In time this will become more conscious. You are at the beginning stages; at the moment the changes are more felt than understood, and this contributes to the fear. People are beginning to come to you for your energy, for who you are spiritually, rather than for your title or your training. They recognise this subconsciously, and you will attract those who need this.

The trouble is that it leaves me feeling a bit isolated from my professional milieu.

You have no need to feel this. You are not isolated from spirit, or from those who come to see you, and to our knowledge the dialogue you have with your community is ceasing to be of any great importance to you anyway. Those colleagues that you do talk to are becoming extremely sympathetic to your methods and approach. The isolation that you experience is that of not having the apparent strength of the professional shell around you. You fear that without it you will not have the same appeal, that your income may be affected. Do not try to return to that which you have practised in the past; this would be regressive. In truth it is beyond your conscious control; it is not what you do that is critical in the work with your clients, it is who you are. We doubt if you will ever truly realise the fullness of who you are in this life; no one ever really does. It is far beyond what you imagine it to be. Trust this.

✡

I am still worried about finances. It is all very well wanting a relationship with spirit and knowing about the Causal plane, but just now it appears that actually having that relationship threatens my livelihood, my training and all that I have worked so hard for. I feel that my spiritual companions almost disparage what I have worked for and accrued in this life.

We do not say that your psychological perspectives and your ways of working are not valued by us; they are. We are asking that you see those perspectives in a larger, spiritual context. Recently you have remarked to others how you have in the past tended to address the spiritual through the psychological, rather than seeing that the spiritual precedes and is greater than the psyche, which is our view. It is a question of hierarchy really, a particular understanding of hierarchy that defines your approach; and this is changing.

Imagine that you are one of the living descendants of a great family, and as in all such cases there comes a time when you inherit the wealth of that family. Now let us assume that your share of the wealth is the family silver, a vast canteen of cutlery. In this canteen are stored all the necessary implements for eating – not just the ordinary day-to-day food but food for special occasions: soupspoons, teaspoons, dessertspoons, serving spoons and ladles, butter knives, fish and steak knives and on and on.

Now, suppose your eyes light on a particularly handsome knife and you pick it up. It works well; it is sharp and has a good balance in the hand. But you would not use it for eating peas or mashed potato, would you? There are other implements within the canteen that are far better suited for these purposes. This knife is a little like psychology: it has a central place within the canteen, but there are other implements too; do not limit yourself to just one. Remember that the purpose of the canteen is to assist nourishment, and this is akin to the spirit that imbues all of the implements.

This image is closer to the truth than you might at first imagine. Spirituality is not the property of one domain or another; it imbues all domains. And every domain addresses the spiritual in one way or another, how can it not? Is not spirit the progenitor of all creation?

In a way this is not so difficult for me to understand. What I find frustrating is more on a personal level: sometimes I see that there is help I can offer from a spiritual dimension, but when I approach the subject it is rejected.

To see is one thing ... You can take a horse to water, but if the horse doesn't drink maybe it is better to wait until it is thirsty. You may see that the horse is dehydrated, but it will not drink until it recognises this for itself. Everyone has their pride and this covers the areas they doubt in themselves; it seals the leaks, in a manner of speaking. When you work with your clients there is an implicit agreement between you that you will assist them in gently prying open the vessel so that they can review and perhaps be more effective in their relationships. They have their expectations, and this to some extent defines what you are able to do. But this is only true of your clients; in all other cases you must operate by different rules.

We feel that these difficulties will evaporate as you truly accept your own spiritual nature. Remember, spirituality does not lie in words, nor in beliefs or actions, although it can imbue all of these. The touch of spirit needs one to ask and another to give. It needs both in order to work, and it will not work without both the creative and the receptive. Spirituality is a quality of being. In a way there is nothing to be done with it except to trust it, and trust that others will see it and call upon it when they need it. You must develop forbearance and patience. Take your cue from us: do we not have to sit back and wait patiently if you cannot find the time or the inclination to meditate? Do you think that we see only the good, the organised, and the true in you? It is not so; we see it all, and all we see we love.

Frankly I find it a rather tall order to love all I see.

If we, too, may be frank, it is not as tall as you think: you do it all the time. We are not asking that you are the same as us; how could you be? We are unencumbered by the travails of life, but in this matter we offer you all our assistance; we charge your heart with love daily. You only have to ask, to think of us, and you will find the inner resources to meet the demands and inconsistencies of your tasks with equilibrium and wisdom. My son, you are not alone; you are with us and we with you. It is only your belief in solitude that makes you falter.

You spend the first half of your life developing control, command and power. Then, just as you feel that you should be reaping the benefits of all the work you have put in, along comes spirit and says, 'No, now you must let go, learn to trust in a greater power.' This is what is happening to you. It is easy to talk of trust, easy to wander through life saying, 'Ah, the universe will provide.' But we are not talking about this superficial sort of trust; the kind of people who subscribe to this view seldom had any power in the first place. You can collapse into spirit or you can continue to live your life as if it does not exist, but neither of these lead anywhere. We are talking of a dynamic, a relationship between two definite, strong poles: yourself and the spiritual personalities you talk to. When this is established my son, the sparks can really fly.

Talk to us.

I don't know what to say. The issues that were burning me up recently don't seem to be so important now.

That is good. Let them sink out of sight. They will not go away, they will bubble away on another level, and thus you are left free to continue your work. There are some things that you can affect and some that are best left to run their course.

Let us speak of soul counselling, of what is meant by this term. What do you understand by it?

Well, if I refer to what I believe is my best work with clients then I think that 'soul counselling' is not very far off the mark. There are times when what I am able to say comes from a deeper place within me. The words are no different from any other time; what is different is where they come from. The emphasis changes. I may refer to the struggle that an individual has had, how difficult their life has been. On other occasions I will refer to their qualities, qualities that perhaps they only half appreciate within themselves. Then again I might point out a new direction, but only if it is true to their nature. Self-appreciation and self-acceptance are common themes; so are accepting their humanness and limitations, being more gentle with themselves. So many people have such unrealistic expectations of themselves and others.

The words are only half the battle. There has to be an opening, and sometimes to create this requires strength or forbearance on my part. It is as if a window opens, a mutual window, and the light from within shines from and towards each other. I think that a great deal of this has to do with an attitude of appreciation, but essentially the opening of this window remains a mystery. On one occasion I can be in the right space and it opens; on another it will not. This indicates to me that the opening is not entirely within my control. The effects when it does open are very often the same: a liberation to spirit and a feeling of timeless depth would be the best way of describing it.

We agree. What opens the window is the soul*, a mutuality of soul, a desire of the soul to dialogue in this way. But there is another window, is there not? The window of the heart. You have only to bear this in mind and the frequency of these events will increase.

✡

* I later developed this theme into an article, much of which was inspired by Malachi, for a small counselling journal. I always felt it deserved a wider read so I have included it in this book as Appendix III!

The 'spiritual' in spiritual counselling is, and always has been, an added ingredient. It is much like your meditation, your inspired channelling, in which the words that you use are from your own life experience but the depth and meaning they are imbued with comes from the spiritual dimension. It is no different with spiritual counselling. But how to achieve it?

Everything starts with a beginning. Nobody gets to the top of the stairs without stepping onto the lower ones first. Take the development of speech in children. At first it is copied from those around them, one word or two; then simple sentences, they broaden their vocabulary, learn to write and read, to communicate with others, learn new ideas and formulations. Then, if it is within the purpose of that life to be inspired by spirit, spirit will begin to bear upon the consciousness of the person, upon their words. But first, the words must be in place, and learned thoroughly. You cannot make verbal inspiration happen. You can wish and wish, but if it is not to be then it will not begin, and you will receive from spirit in a different way.

With counselling it is the same. First you learn the craft, a good basic training with examples to copy. Then you practise your craft, then you go beyond that craft. To go beyond that craft you need, to some extent, to surrender in trust. The point we are making is that all development is sequential; there are no magic paths, no mystical transformations, no short cuts or sudden changes. The road is traversed by starting at the beginning and putting one foot in front of the other, each step building on the last. There is no fast track to spiritual wisdom, it takes a lifetime of work and only bears fruit in the later years.

Now this is also true of your clients. It is no good talking of the finer points of theology to someone who is in deep emotional pain because their partner has left them. First you must repair; you must address their needs in their own language, but from a spiritual perspective, and this requires real talent. To couch spiritual truths in a way that is practical without becoming trite is a matter of flair and experience. To actually be open to your own inspiration while being confronted with deep emotional trauma is a skill which requires years and years of practice. The very nature of the dialogue between client and counsellor actually works against spiritual inspiration, but it can be done.

If you want your spirit guides to help you, you must ask them, but not during the session, when it is too late. A brief meditation, a prayer before you start, will be sufficient. If you can say this in front of your client, even having them join in, it will be even more effective.

✡

Tell us what you find most helpful when you are in need, when you are the one who is being counselled.

Understanding.

And how is this understanding communicated to you?

Nuance, energy, attitude and words, the way in which they are spoken. In fact the orientation of the counsellor is irrelevant.

So it is, and there you have the secret. You cannot counsel spiritually at the same time as hanging on to all the precepts of psychology. You have to let them be and go beyond them. Think of your mentation as a small savings account rather than the source of abundance. So many hang on to their savings, their precious ideas, for dear life, and what do they have at the end of the day? Exactly what they started with plus a little meagre interest. If they would just realise that their savings are nothing more than a glass of water taken from a vast and gentle river. Empty your glass and it will always refill, refill with fresh water, fresh ideas that are from the river; empty it and it will fill again. Hoard what you have and it will become stale and repetitive, cut off from the source, you understand? The river is the heart, the voice of the soul, constant and yet ever-changing; your ideas catch the sparkles reflected from the surface, they do not produce them.

✡

There is an energy now in place, an energy that you can rely upon to inform you and your work, if you trust it. We could say that this energy comes from us but that would not be quite accurate; but neither does it come from yourself alone. It is more of a marriage, a cooperation at a very subtle level. Believe us when we say that there is a harbour, protected from the seas of uncertainty and confusion. It is in those calm waters that the Masters dwell. They see your approach; they wait with anticipation for you to arrival. You are not far from it, not far at all. Listen now, as your beloved Yeshua tells you himself:

> Dear brother, my own interest lies in expanding your understanding of the breadth of spiritual reality, in helping to elevate your consciousness into the spiritual realm. You are now removing the bricks from the wall that separates you from spirit very quickly; the mortar is loose, crumbling, the bricks separate easily and you are within sight of your goal. When you reach it you will see clearly what has always been there, what has always surrounded you. In truth nothing will change but your awareness, but what an important step, what an important recognition! That homecoming is the realisation that you never left, you simply glanced away. I am just the light on the shore toward which you are heading. You follow my beacon because you can, but truly, as you are at sea, so you stand beside me.

From the sublime to the mundane. A few days later I am once again suffering some pretty serious financial anxieties, I fear that I am going to lose everything.

Each day brings new opportunities, each dawn new possibilities. Every morning a fresh start. There is very little in your world that is continuous; you live in a state of change, a state of flux, ever-changing. It has been said that the only thing that is constant is change, but change does not always have to be for the worse. Recent experiences are leading you to expect this, to fear it and thus to command it to be so. We cannot take away the anxiety that is created by lack of money, but we can tell you how to attract resources to yourself. It is through positive thinking – yes, and before you groan that you have heard it all before, it is through positive visualisation. It is through ascertaining the movement of the tides and sailing with them rather than against them. This you are starting to do.

Psychology is ebbing; the days of the analyst are numbered. What will come in their place are those things that you have already divined, cooperation with spirit in psychological healing. It will be twenty years or more before this starts to be accepted but there will be those who will come to walk with you towards those goals. Every building starts with the laying of one stone. You have laid your stone and laid it well, so such privation as you suffer is not for no purpose.

✡

It is not easy to speak with Malachi each day. It is always a pleasure in the moment but the effects are not always what I expect. The ongoing theme seems to be a reduction of 'me'. In truth I don't think it is a reduction at all but rather the placing of my identity in a much larger context and reality. But knowing this doesn't stop the feeling.

It is not only the time of cessation of the personal; it is also a time of spiritual increase within you. We say this to you, but it is just as important for those people who approach you for your counsel. As the attachment to the personal wanes the ability to ingest the spiritual waxes.

Imagine yourself to be in a distant part of the land, untouched by civilisation, born to a simple family, who have perhaps farmed the same piece of land for generations. Your needs are simple, your pleasures are simple, you eat the food you grow and what you do not grow you do not eat. Perhaps you have a few animals and you are more or less content with your life except for one thing: a longing to know of the greater world that exists beyond the area where you live.

So you set off. You take it upon yourself to travel, and after many months you come upon a great city, the centre of administration for the whole land, filled with culture, wealth, and poverty. You wander, lost, bewildered, perhaps even laughed at for your simple ways, and before long you start to long for the old ways, the basic ways of your life in the country with your family, with the certainty of the seasons to guide you. You become depressed, frightened; perhaps you become angry and you rebel against this great institution. But you know that here is knowledge that you could never find at home.

It is like this with those who seek spirit: to realise that you are one subject within a kingdom rather than the kingdom itself is not easy; it evokes fear and fear evokes in some a reaction to the kingdom. To be one tiny speck of sand on the beach, vulnerable to the vagaries of the tides, rather than imagining yourself to be lord of the beach itself is quite a demand, we realise this. But those specks of sand which are humanity have a unique capacity. As well as being part of the beach, they can stand above it, see and recognise their place and part within the greater scheme of things, and know that without that place and part, the scheme would be diminished. It is a paradox: in truth you are lords and yet at the same time you are no more than specks of sand within creation. A difficult paradox to overcome!

Those who seek spirit gradually have their beliefs and attachments challenged. Those things that have got you so far, that you have come to rely upon, are now being questioned by you, and this is because of your involvement in this path. But spirit is never in opposition to personal history. It embraces it, it exalts it; for your experience and your history are what the beach is made of. Without them there would be nothing for the waves of spirit to caress.

✡

I have been praying that my talents, such as they are, will be put to greater use. The population of my practice is continuing to thin out. I am enjoying the time and space that this gives me but at the same time it raises financial anxieties. With ninety per cent of my income spoken for in mortgage and running expenses, losing ten per cent accounts for the disposable part and leaves me practically skint. So I do what I can practically to increase my income, pray to God and ask my Higher Self for assistance.

Do not fear for your counselling work. The places that are vacant will soon be taken up again, but you have within you a need to rest, a need to recharge. Think of this as a time of change, of transformation and of inner rebuilding. It takes time – time and peace to recharge. It will pass. We can assure you that your talents will not go to waste and neither will you starve to death.

There is little we can do save to bring you healing. Just relax [*I feel a softening in my body, like a warm, relaxing breeze*]. There, it will strengthen your purpose and bring you peace.

The shape and style of your work is changing, and this is the desire of your soul. If you look closely at what is going on you will see that it is not just the population of your practice that is changing but the needs of those who come; you will see that they are coming for less time and with less frequency. Over the coming months and years this will develop even more; you will see far more people than you currently see, but on a less protracted basis. They will come for perhaps one visit or two, then again later for one more visit and so on. It is your ability that is enabling this rather than your lack of it. It is quite unusual to be able to add a truly spiritual dimension to the purely psychological, but this you are managing to do. It makes the work extremely effective.

It will take time for people to recognise these talents but your abilities will become known and sought out. Many, many psychologists and counsellors feel that they are unable to reach the hearts of their clients; they stick to formulas and understandings that discourage this. Those who work from a spiritual perspective often feel helpless to address the deeply human contradictions and compulsions of those they speak with, but you, my son, can do both. This ability is in its infancy but we feel that if you look back over the years, even over the last six months, you will see that this is what you have been working towards for so long. Those you help will speak to others and they will come; your practice will re-build and your work will become known in the same way as it has in the past, but what you will become known for will be different from that which has gone before. What you do will be seen as even more personal and unique to you, original rather than of one theoretical school or another. We feel that this is already happening, has been happening for some years now; but there comes a point when it is impossible to stand in the old camp any longer, you have to step into the new. But do not turn your back on the old camp completely; your training, your study and experience are your foundations and you have built them well.

Do trust; return the faith that the Creator has put in you by putting your faith in Him. If you can do this then we can assure you that all will be well.

Chapter 6

The turning of the age

Nobody can predict the outcome of those events and changes that are about to take place on the planet and amongst humanity. The turning of an age, every two thousand years, always brings with it both tragedy and opportunity. But it is probably safe to say that, as with every other crisis situation, some will move forward, embrace those tragedies and learn from them, while others will flee and turn against one another. There will be death, not so much in the far north where you live, but in the more southerly hemispheres there will be death. The sand and the earth will rise up and then the waters of the seas will wash over and make everything clean again. When these things happen people will ask why. Some of the scientists will understand that this has been brought about by man himself, but scientists will only be able to answer some of the questions. People will turn to the ancient wisdom for answers, to philosophy, to God. Not so much to religion, no – its force is almost spent. It will be the Aquarian children that will come, the Children of Light, and they will bring their influence and understanding to bear, They will help those that survive to build a sustainable world based on spiritual principles. People will not resist them; we feel that they will have little left to lose.

✡

In time to come there will be ample opportunity to meditate. Meditation, contemplation, reflection will take a far higher precedence than they do today. This will in part be because people will not require the sheer quantity of material possessions that they currently do, and thus will not have to give all the hours of their day to work. More importantly, meditation will be recognised as the most important form of progression that humankind can participate in. Historians will rely more and more on past life memory for their information. Every age has its keynote, that which man values. In the Piscean Age it was science; in the Aquarian it will first be the connection with God, then seeking to have that connection reflected in the world and the behaviour of man. Heaven on earth will be the goal of the Aquarian children. There will not be anything like the degree of distraction you suffer when you sit in your early morning reverie, with the pressure of the upcoming day, the aircraft noise outside your window or the tiredness that so often afflicts those who live in industrialised cities. In the Aquarian future God will once again take His place upon His throne in the minds of humanity and man once again will recognise that but for the grace of God there would be no creation.

✡

As you have been told, the Millennium brings with it a completely new energy. The archangel Uriel is moving out with the Piscean age and the archangel Michael is entering with the Aquarian. Michael will bring unimagined possibilities: changes in science, spirituality and the way people live their lives. This will not happen immediately, of course, but gradually, over a long period of time.

So what does it mean to stand in this new energy? It means to feel the new coursing through your being. It means being surprised by your own responses to situations; it means opening to a new set of priorities. These new ways of seeing things are already within you, but they are not uppermost, not the first that you would turn to in a given situation. It is like any breakthrough, in science, in the arts or philosophy. People for years consider one thing to be a certain way. They stake their lives and reputations on it being that way, until somebody comes along and says, 'No, it is not like that, it is like this!' And they are opposed by those who have an investment in the old way, but gradually they give way, they see the sense in the argument and they move. None can ultimately stand against progress.

For many years humankind believed that the earth was flat and that the sun revolved around it. They lived perfectly contentedly with this understanding until one man came along and said, 'It is not so.' And he was opposed. It did not make any difference to the way people lived their lives on a daily basis; they still had to cook, work, feed their children. What it did do was to enable other possibilities to come to people's minds about the nature of humanity in relation to the universe. So even when the new is spoken it is seldom the first truth that changes things. The first truth is like the opening of a door; passing through it comes later. So when we talk about standing in the new we mean opening to that new energy, that new breeze that is not tired, that is fresh and brings new possibilities in its wake, that will cause you to be engaged, energised and intrigued by what you are doing. It will bring you pleasure and satisfaction; this is how you will know it.

✡

There is, within the workings of human life, a factor of resistance. Not just within the individual or the individual's environment so much as between the two. It is there for all; it is as intrinsic to life as the need to breathe. Many, many things affect this factor. The movements of the heavenly spheres, the attitudes of the individuals upon the planet, the needs of the individual's community, the political, the cultural and the movements of spirit – they all bear on this factor.

There are very few people who are finding this current transition easy. Those things that people have been able to rely upon for many years, that they have expected to be reliable for the rest of their lives, are simply not there. This is leading to great confusion, great questioning and soul-searching. Those things are not there because they are no longer useful, they are no longer needed. They are slowly being replaced by new things, and these will be seen and recognised by new people, the young and those who do not bring the expectations of the past with them.

Of all generations, the generation for whom life is most difficult at this point in time are those in their middle years. The elderly are more philosophical; they have seen more change throughout their lives, and are not so dependent on work to provide for their families. The young know no better and accept life as it is given. It goes without saying – and always has done – that humanity must adapt to survive. Those who adapt will be those that make a success. But it is not so easy: what to adapt *to* is the question.

Ultimately that which humanity values will change. It will not so be much the material product that is valued, or the labour, the sheer labour that is valued. It will be quality and wisdom that people will come to covet. But it may be many years before this asserts itself. In the meantime humanity is caught in the crosscurrent. The wind blows people on shore, the tide pulls them away; anxiety and stasis set in. But time itself will make changes; in time one direction will become the stronger and the path forward will become clear.

Chapter 7

Malachi's life

You asked about my life, the life of Malachi. I understand that subsequent to my death I have been given the rather grandly diminished title of 'lesser prophet'. So now, step within me and see things through the eyes of a lesser prophet.

I can see pale dusty rocks, hot sun, dry. I am in the mountains in the hot sun, walking with a stick or staff. I have a very full beard, dark curly hair, long. I am a little lame in my left leg, a slight limp. The path passes through a gully between two very large sections of rock, shaded and cool as I walk through. The gully exits out onto some sort of plateau that overlooks a huge valley. In the valley there is a river and a city, fields surrounding it full of green, a vast basin. I am standing looking out over it.

This is my world. I walk; I love walking in the mountains with nothing to support me but my stick and the kindness of those I meet on the way. This is where I contemplate, I walk and I think. This is my meditation, this is where God speaks to me, while I am walking.

History dignifies experience because it is written with the benefit of hindsight, long after the life in question has been weighed in the balance, but I was no different from you. I was just a man, with my meditations and the whispering of a God that I could hardly believe. I, too, had to expose those precious words to people who mocked, argued or felt that they knew better. Perhaps it was easier for me, people then knew less and needed more.

✡

I am with Malachi and he is taking me along a dusty, pale coloured path. It is extremely hot, it must be the middle of the day, but there is a breeze of thin air about us as we walk. We come to a clearing, climbing over tumbled rock and scree, to massive boulders around a small plateau. Malachi squats, looking intently at the sand in front of him. Young and slim, dark black beard and long curled hair, head cocked to one side as if he is listening. I can see the olive skin of his face turning white at his neck; long, slim fingers wipe the sweat from his face with his headcloth.

He gestures me to squat and I do so. It is hot and painful and uncomfortable, but I remain motionless like Malachi. He puts his finger to his lips and points to his ear. The heat and the silence are stifling. He closes his eyes and is lost inside himself, swaying very slightly on his heels, his head cocked to one side.

Then I hear it too ... the faintest, high pitched hum, as if the rocks themselves are singing. It is an extremely gentle and reassuring sound ... I know now why he has brought me here. He whispers to me that this sound is the sound of God, it is the sound of creation. It has always been; so much has come and gone while this has remained constant. 'You too,' he says, 'have come, will have your day and be gone, and when you are gone this is what will remain.'

✡

I see all around me the light, pinkish-cream coloured rocks. I hear the crunch of Malachi's sandal in the gravel as he turns on the path to face me. He is quite young, not a boy, a man. His hair is black; long oily curls frame his weather-beaten face. He is hot, sweating, dirty, his tunic open at the front. He has been working hard. He is with a fairly large number of sheep, over fifty, maybe as many as a hundred, corralled in a natural pen in the rocks. With him are two or three other men; he is quite commanding, yells to them what he wants. He makes his way through the sheep, gripping them by the coat and turning them to the side as he goes. He is searching among the sheep until he sees what he wants, a newborn, a lamb with its mother.

I can feel his feelings, as if I were him. He hardens his heart, lifts the lamb out of the flock; it bleats shrilly, and the soft calling of the mother is ringing in his ears. He holds the lamb to his chest gently but firmly, as it struggles to be free, the soft, tight curls of its coat against his skin, so perfect and so vulnerable. He has taken the best. Young, perfectly formed and full of life. He tells himself that this lamb belongs to God and walks numbly towards the entrance to the pen.

I see him standing before me now, his eyes are dark, wild, beautiful and deep. He speaks to me.

This is how we gave sacrifice when I walked the earth, always the best lamb or the best sheep, and many times it fell to me to choose. It was not just a case of blood being spilled but of experiencing all the feelings; they were all an important part of the sacrifice, from the choosing to the separation and the actual killing. We gave to God what gave us life. We gave to God our feelings. Our God was a God of wrath, a God that ruled the seasons and Who had to be appeased lest we all starved. We worshipped our God in the way we understood.

Your God is a God of love, so what will you sacrifice? A lamb will not do, and throwing your possessions away is point-less. My brother, you must sacrifice all within you that resists love, all within you that argues with love. It is not so difficult. The arms of love are tender, they are forgiving and they are within you, just as He is within you, just as God is within you, there is no separation save that which you create. Place it all on the altar and let it burn.

✡

I re-experience the following in the present, as if I were Malachi.

It has been an awful night, a difficult and dark night. I spent it at my home, a single-storey dwelling built in the traditional manner within our family compound. Our family is large and supports many people and their families, so my work today is of importance, not just to me but to the whole community. I am up before dawn, there is much to do today. It is a feast day and a great many people are up like I am, preparing food and drink. My task is to prepare the sacrifice.

I am gathering wood for the sacrificial fire from a store set aside for this purpose. There are no thick logs but branches which are not of particularly high quality, thin and very dry; I have to break and cut them into uniform lengths and bind them into bundles. There is a specific way of doing this and prayers must be said before and after. Now they are stacked neatly.

I am inspecting the knife. It must be very sharp indeed; in matters of sacrifice the sharpest cut is the kindest cut, hardly felt by the animal. All they know is their life slipping back to the Creator, like going to sleep.

It is later in the day and I am carrying my little charge towards the altar. It is a large, flat topped-stone a short way outside the compound, set upon it are the bundles I prepared earlier with a tallow candle burning smokily alongside. Sur-rounding the stone are the men and boys of our community. They part to let me through. What I must do must be done with the utmost solemnity, and I walk slowly and deliberately. I nod to an assistant who sets a flame to the wood. It sputters into life; it has been dressed liberally with fat and oil.

Gently I lift the lamb above my head, and those assembled fall silent. It is quite still in my hands. I lower it to the ground and quickly cut its throat with the knife, the blood warm on my hand. I feel the little one's life slip away as I speak the words that are needed at this stage. I stand and raise the body above my head. I pause and there is a mutter of approval from the crowd; then I commit the corpse to the flames. I say the required words and step back from the altar to indicate that my work is done. The tension breaks. The relief amongst all who are assembled is palpable and they start to talk excitedly among themselves. I take my leave quietly and go to bathe in the manner that is prescribed.

✡

In every experience there is a downward spiral and an upward spiral. So in each experience a choice is presented, a choice which you would call interpretation but which in truth is a movement of energy within the experience itself. Thus you may make something positive of that experience or you may make something negative of it. Something positive would be to learn, to understand, to deepen your compassion. Something negative would be to reinforce a poor self-image or prove to yourself that a partial view is a total one. I was confronted with the negative many times in my own life, and these events were exacerbated by my fundamentally angry rather than forgiving nature.

I see an image of Malachi holding what appears to be quite a large scroll. He is unwinding it and showing me what is written on it.

This scroll represents the teachings that were given to me by the elders and which I took to myself. Now these teachings brought me into conflict with myself. When one seeks teachings one is looking for something which is not immediately of the self; why would you look outside yourself for teachings if they were accessible within? So you seek something more and what you find does not always immediately bring what you were hoping for, does not always bring peace. I took these teachings to myself and some were like swallowing pieces of sharp flint, they were hard for me to digest. They did not illuminate my experience but caused within me a need for self-discipline, to discipline those areas within myself that did not fit with the teaching. And so my scrolls eventually became more comfortable to carry.

As soon as teachings have been sought and accepted they create this tension; you become two rather than one. There are the teachings, so high and pure, and there are your human failings, so painful to see. Here you have much of what has been occurring in your life. You have sought the teachings, you have imbibed them, you speak them, and yet you are a hypocrite. You are a hypocrite and seen to be so by others and yourself because you cannot yet live those teachings. I understand what an uncomfortable position this is to be in.

✡

The next few scenes are viewed through Malachi's eyes. The first came just before.I set off on a spiritual retreat.

I can see our compound on the plain below. Beyond that are hills leading to mountains soft and misty in the distance; above me is an enormous blue sky. I take a last look over my shoulder and I turn and make my way into the mountains, away from home. I am travelling with a staff, a skin of water and a very thick, warm cloak made of animal skin; it is rolled and I carry it across my back. As usual I have very mixed feelings about leaving my family.

In amongst the rocks and gorges there is more shade; it is cooler and I start to feel more comfortable about being alone. I start to enjoy the stillness and silence of the mountains. After a morning of walking I sit with my back to a rock and my thoughts come like falling stars, each one gently bursting within my mind, revealing the truth, revealing the mind of God.

✡

Behind me there are some trees, still in the hot sun; they are fruit trees, a grove of lemon trees. They are not very big and the yield of fruit is poor like the ground they are planted in, poor farming land – and where the land is poor the harvest is subjected even more than normally to the vagaries of the weather. I am walking along to a small settlement, one or two scrawny chickens at my feet, an old woman peering from the darkness of a doorway as I pass. I find the dwelling I am looking for and hesitate for a moment before I call a man's name. He pulls aside the cloth at the door and bids me enter. The room has no furnishing, and an earthen floor, but for all its poverty the beds are tidy around the walls. My host bids me to be seated and his wife brings some hot tea. On the ground between us she places a wooden plate on which are some small ripe figs and nuts. He pushes the plate towards me and urges me to eat. I take a fig; it is soft and sweet.

There are so many social protocols to be observed, all the more so because we are not of the same wealth, not of the same standing in the community. He asks after my family and I after his, while outside the sun beats down relentlessly. There has been no rain for months; we are in the midst of a drought. And this man, our neighbour, offers me the figs that he has gathered and that are probably the only food he has. Although I have eschewed wealth personally our family has great store. I take my leave. We have not discussed directly his plight – we have not had to, I have been immersed in it. When I get back to our home I will arrange for some of our supplies to be sent to him on a regular basis until the rains soften the soil.

✡

It is hot, the ground is powdery and dry. I can feel the brittle dusty leaves of an olive tree next to my face. I am standing amongst these mean and twisted trees to take advantage of the little shade they afford. Stretched out in front of me is a vast shimmering desert, so hot that it looks like a sea. Beyond the desert in the distance, are blue mountains.

I am not naturally drawn to the desert. Every man has his landscape, for some it is the sea, for some the lakes, while some love the cultivated land. I am drawn to the mountains, but on this occasion I must enter the desert, so still, so empty; it confronts the soul in an entirely different way from the mountains. I am here on a quest, to rid myself of all that which is not worthy of me.

✡

Truly there is no end, even death is not an end. That was the
lesson that Yeshua came to teach humankind, that after
death life continues in another dimension, and that love, above
all else, is the most important thing that humanity can aspire to.
My life was long and I did not fully realise the truth of what I
have just said until near the end. Come now, walk with me, a
very old, weary prophet, and tell me of your troubles.

✡

*I can see Malachi, His full beard grey and thin, he is very frail.
He gestures to me to join him and we walk together, as usual along
a mountain path. We walk until we reach a high promontory from
which the view is breathtaking. Below us is the valley in which he
lives; before us the valley opens into the plains and beyond them, the
desert. Above us an azure sky, the heat of the sun beating down.
We stand between heaven and earth, the air clear and cool, far
below us the eagles wheel in the sky. 'Malachi, I am so afraid for
the future.' He nods. After a few moments he inclines his head
slightly towards me without taking his eyes from the vista and says
with great gentleness:*

You have quite a task ahead of you. There is no room for the
fainthearted, so let what is fainthearted within you step
back. Draw strength from the strong, from all that is strong
within you, you understand? Draw strength from the strong.
Do this and all will be well.

✡

*The final passage of this chapter is the most intense identification
with Malachi that I have had. I actually became him and felt his
fatigue, his pain and age in my body during the visualisation.*

I am leaning heavily on a staff, bony hands gripping, shaking
as I place it a few inches in front of me with each step. My
body is weary and filled with pain. My eyes are not what they
used to be and I can only just see the path in front of me. I carefully place one foot in front of the other in case I fall. If I did,
it would not be the first time and it would make them reluctant
to let me out again. They worry about me hurting myself. I

cannot get so far these days but they indulge me as long as I stay close to the buildings. Today I have the pleasure of walking with some of the little ones, my grandchildren. They lift my heart so much.

I stop and lean on a rock; if only I could get my breath! I look down at the top of my stick, faithful friend, polished from countless years of being held. One of my little companions climbs up beside me chattering, oblivious to the great ache and fatigue that life has imparted to my ancient frame. Like a mist, my suffering and self-absorption evaporate into the beauty and gaiety of her laughter.

I am not long for this world: sometimes I can hardly remember who I am. I know that I have learned much during my stay here, although if you asked me what it was I could not say. What surprises me is that I go on learning; there is no respite from learning, always something new to understand. I am here now, the living embodiment of the past, and sitting next to me laughing is the future. The fact that I can recognise this seems to me to be a reflection of what was once an organised mind and it pleases me to think it.

When I was younger I thought that I was important, that what I did and said would make a difference. Maybe it did, but that doesn't matter now. It is not the detail of life that is important; it is the relationship of that detail to a greater scheme of things that counts. Not me but my relationship to God: that is all that matters. When the meal has been prepared and eaten, the cups drained and the stories told, that is the only thing that remains. It is the only thing that is constant, that has always been and always will be. Like the soft evening sun, that great, patient, forgiving light which bathes me now and says with infinite love, 'When you are ready Malachi ...'

And I reply, 'Just a little longer, Lord, with the children.'

Chapter 8

Malachi's prophecies

God provided man with all he needed for his comfort and left it in the charge of humanity. Now humankind has brought about a situation in which the planet is changing, and these changes will not always bring comfort. It is not God's fault; God created the laws of nature but cannot enforce them. It is the thoughts and deeds of man which have created problems. But just as they have created problems, they can solve them. If there is a realisation of error, a change in attitude, individually as well as globally, then those predictions we make may not occur. Our predictions are based upon what will happen if there is no change.

This year there will be a loss of water stocks due to the heat of the sun. Also, paradoxically, it is expected that there will be severe flooding in certain places. We cannot say exactly where, but there will be drought in some areas and flooding in others. [*In fact this turned out to be a year of drought in England and flooding on the continent.*]

We tell you this so that you are forewarned, so that you can develop trust in the more concrete statements we make. We find that the best way to facilitate this is for us to inform you of what will be happening, and then for you to observe the events themselves. In this way you will come to believe our predictions and if the time comes when we must warn you of dire circumstances approaching, you will have trust in our words; you will be able to inform those who will listen.

Now, we will step aside so that Yeshua may talk with you for a few moments.

My brother, life when I was upon the earth was not dissimilar from your own. There is very little to compare between the feelings of doubt, insufficiency and powerlessness. You look to the vision and then you look back to yourself; the gap seems so large. It felt to me, too, that what was being asked of me was impossible; that I had neither the talents nor the resources to meet the demand.

I had no money, I had no temple, I had no particular organisation. All I had was the love of my family, my feet with which to travel, my hands with which to heal and my voice to speak. Then and now are not so different. There were those then who would wait for money, for groups to step forward, for buildings, for permission from the authorities. But you, too, have the love of your teachers; you have your feet, your hands and your voice to use. If you work with what you have, the rest will follow.

✡

When I, Malachi, and those of us who are your main inspirers, walked the surface of the earth, there were things we could take for granted, the things that we loved and carried with us, the things that we ate – all far more simple than they are today. But in essence there is not so much difference; the inner feeling of man is much the same. When we talk with you we find those things which concern you to be not so dissimilar from those things which concerned us: providing for your family, wanting to make a contribution to the good of humanity in some way. But all this requires stability in the world and this stability is not something that your generation can easily take for granted.

We feel that if the great waves come – and they will come if mankind does not act quickly to stop them – it will be a great test. A great many will be carried home on those waves, carried home to the spirit realms. Those that remain will be faced with destruction: the great cities that have been built, that seem so permanent and so strong, will be nothing when faced with the might of the oceans. Then people's values will have to change; perhaps then humankind will begin to understand what a privilege it is to worry for the future of their children. Perhaps then the beauty of simplicity will begin to be appreciated once again.

✡

Great and deep will be the suffering of the humanity: disease, pestilence, tidal waves, earthquakes and volcanoes. Cause and effect, not the work of God. If you light the fuse, does not the dynamite explode? The fuse has been lit by greed, and greed has been stimulated by fear, and fear is what is left when love has been thrown out of the human heart.

It does not have to be so. Even now it can be changed, changed in an instant by thought alone. But who can spare a thought for humanity as a whole when their own need is so powerful? Who can spare a thought for the whole, for their brothers, for their sisters, for the gentle animals who are their companions and for the earth under their feet?

Who can afford not to? The world is in your hands, nobody else's. God and the spirit realms can do nothing except through humanity. We have no power save through those who will listen to the quiet voice in their hearts, those who will shed a tear for what they see around them.

✡

Man has taken so much without giving back. What gardener would expect soil to continue to support plants without ever putting anything back into that earth? None would. And yet this is how humankind are treating the planet. They don't even bother to clear up the remains of their industry, their mines and their factories when they have ceased to be profitable; they are just left to rot.

It cannot go on, but it will not be God who will stop it. God cannot do this, God does not have that power. It will be the laws of balance which man has chosen to ignore that will seek redress, and the laws of balance are all-powerful and utterly impartial. They are not to be trifled with; they will not say, 'This one recycled their waste so they can be spared.' They will simply recreate things in a way that will enable the planet to recover. The pendulum can only swing so far in one direction before it starts to swing back.

It took millions upon millions of years to create the resources of the planet and it has taken scarcely five hundred to deplete those resources to a dangerous level. Humankind were never meant to dominate nature, they were meant to live in harmony with it, and if they had done so nature would have given freely and effortlessly for as long as they needed. But no, fear and greed became the gods of man and he has worshipped them without restraint.

But all is not lost. If humankind can start to honour the Lord of Creation again there will still be a chance, because the Lord of Creation is also the Lord of Love, and love dissolves fear, dissolves greed and envy as surely as the warmth of the sun melts ice.

✡

The Book of Malachi

To understand the book of Malachi, that which appears in the Holy Book, it is necessary to understand the time in which I lived. The ageless wisdom is just that, but the vessel into which it is poured is shaped by the time and the needs and the awareness of the people of that time. The practices that I, Malachi, spoke of in the Holy Book were practices that those I spoke to could understand and relate to. Yet, as you have understood, they are also metaphors which lay the ground in consciousness for the realisation of the God within. The prophets of the Old Testament were very great men; they practised many observances, and experienced much discipline in order to achieve the purity of mind required to speak what they understood to be the voice of the Lord.

Always the prophets speak the same message, and that message is to remind humanity of the omnipresence of God, to remind humanity that God the Creator created both laws and free will. Much of the work of the prophets was as a preparation, helping humanity, and particularly the Jews, to understand the depth, the breadth and the height of their existence. The Jews were a poor people in the time when I lived, driven by need, survival and fear. It did not take much to set one against the other, each desiring to dominate the other in order to have a better advantage.

It was into this community that I was born, and to these circumstances that I spoke, but knowing a different truth: that God both created abundance, and gave humanity a gift. That gift was to know God as no other had before. In truth, the people to whom I spoke were far closer to their instincts than people are now. They understood actions rather than ideas, so the act of sacrificing that which enabled their survival was a very direct way of going beyond the self to something greater.

✡

I have been doing some research on Malachi. I suspect Old Testament scholars may argue with my interpretations but this is what I have gleaned. He is the last of the prophets in the Old Testament; his prophesy is fairly short compared with some but it has some features that mark it out, notably that he is the first and only OT prophet to refer to God as Father. Some commentators suggest that this in itself foreshadowed the coming Christ. The third chapter of his work provides the basis for the most beautiful passages of Handel's Messiah.

At first reading Malachi seems to be berating the priests for having fallen and become corrupt and the people for bringing unsound sacrifices to the altar. This is not unusual in the OT prophecies, but on closer reading, looking at the symbolism of the words, he is speaking of much deeper truths:

He affirms that God loves the Jews (the chosen ones).
He questions the power of the priests (implying that they do not follow the Law).
He berates the people for not giving the best to God.
He reminds people that God is Lord of all (entreating people to live by the Law).
He berates duplicity and admonishes fallen priests.
He entreats people to follow God, not Mammon.
He stands against a lack of discrimination.
He prophesies the coming of the Messiah.
He berates people for believing in the illusion of their omnipotence.
He talks of the laws of cause and effect.
He prophesies the coming of Elijah and the Children of Light.

As I read the passages in the Bible I gained a deeper understanding of the significance of sacrifice in the barbaric times of the prophets. I felt that to Malachi the altar represents a sort of portal in space and time through which man can commune with God.

It may seem prosaic, but sacrificing animals (which represented wealth and more importantly survival) on the altar is perhaps a metaphor for diminishing the animal self, thus increasing the capacity for the divine. Bhudda realised that the cause of suffering is attachment, and attachment is in turn to do with the survival instinct, which in turn again is amplified by the belief that we are finite beings, of the earth alone. I think that perhaps the altar of the body is the heart, which is the linking point between the human and the divine.

The prophets were in a way precursors to the Christ. They spoke the words of the Christos; they felt that they spoke the words of God, whereas Yeshua embodied the will of God. This was also true to some extent of Elijah. Malachi himself was a healer of sorts as well as a prophet; he was very aware of the healing power of words.

The Higher Self, Soul and Reincarnation

Initially soul was one vast energy field. At a particular point in evolution this exploded into a myriad particles which gathered together into Higher Selves. The Master has often said that it is difficult to explain the true nature of the Higher Self. Language itself is based on what individuals see around them and it is difficult to understand what cannot be perceived.

Each individual soul is an aspect or particle of a Higher Self, and each Higher Self contains more particles than there are cells in a human body. Not all aspects incarnate, just as a woman has the potential to conceive hundreds of children in a lifetime but may only actually give birth to two or three children. At the end of life the individualised soul returns to the Higher Self and the experiences and learning of that life is shared throughout the entire Higher Self. Once an aspect has incarnated it cannot return; each aspect or cell of the Higher Self can only incarnate once. Because of this, when a soul returns, something akin to a conference takes place when the karma is reviewed. The experiences and understanding of that life are evaluated and a new aspect steps forward, with the essence of the previous life within, to take the learning forward.

If the Higher Self could be seen, it would resemble a vast rainbow. The particles that comprise it are organised according to the colours of that rainbow, called light streams – pink, amethyst, gold, silver, green and blue and all the hundreds of shades in between. Each light stream has a different learning pattern and this pattern typically takes two to three hundred incarnations to fulfil; also each Higher Self has an average of over one thousand light streams within it. The Master defined a light stream in the following way:

'A light stream, or directional light particle, is an impulse of combined energy factors which permit the soul to choose and travel along a particular path of endeavour towards enlightenment. It is that which gives the ability for attainment mentally and intellectually, while the soul is in the limited confines of matter.'

The Higher Self can incarnate more than one individualised soul at a time. Usually they don't meet, but sometimes in the later stages of spiritual development souls that share a Higher Self incarnate as members of the same family.

Apparently if one could view the Higher Self one would be delighted by its great beauty. Joseph of Arimathea has said:

'Imagine looking at a sunset, how the sky above radiates the light, how each cloud represents a facet of the pinks and oranges, the blues and greens of the sunset; and then imagine the Higher Self.

'Some may say, "But if the soul has such proportions how is there room for so many in spirit?" But spirit is not measured by an area of space; spirit is a dimension. It is not like your world where you must travel from one place to another in order to experience the change of view, the different countries and the people dwelling in them. Spirit, being a dimension of light, contains all things in a relatively small area in comparison with your world. Unfortunately, to be able to visualise that which you have never seen is virtually impossible.'

So a true insight into the Higher Self – the total soul – can never be achieved because it is of a vastly different vibration from that of which the body is aware.

The soul has the opportunity to learn in spirit as well as upon the earth. But the earth is an important school for the soul, where the Higher Self can enrich its understanding with first-hand knowledge of the full range of human emotions. Ultimately it is where the Higher Self can come to know love. It is the planet where the soul can express itself, can move forward and has that greatest blessing of all – free will. The soul in its own environment does not have free will. It has total knowledge and understanding of life and universal law; it has accepted what it is simply to be; but that is not sufficient for truly understanding the lessons that life can offer, lessons such as compassion, tolerance, understanding and patience.

When the soul enters the physical self at the time of birth, conscious knowledge of the past is concealed. Later, at different times of life, an aspect of the Higher Self that has lived before, and that has an interest or karmic investment in the particular events or lessons that are being lived through, will step forward to offer help, assistance and understanding. This help is often initially recognised through synchronicity, experiences of *déjà vu* or dreaming. Through meditation and spiritual development such a link with a 'spirit guide' can be built upon and parts of the past life can even be recalled. The spiritually-enhanced understanding of the guide can then help the individual to go forward, develop and succeed.

The voice of soul

I wrote this article for a small psychological journal. It contains a great deal of Malachi's influence and I have included it here as an addendum to chapter 5.

The quiet slog of therapy, with no quick fixes, just consistent work through the long months of summer, through the grey toil of winter, through laughter and anger, through sadness and loss, through desire and indifference, love and longing, accusation and criticism, scorn, pleading, pleasing, wheedling and boredom. Across the floor of my consulting room march the scorned armies of the psyche – wounded, denied, rejected and rationalised. One at a time I greet them, one at a time we hear them, listen to their pain, listen to the fragment of truth that they have carried and protected for so long. It is such hard work, such painstaking work. Who can blame those who give up and leave?

Some leave to find a better therapist, some blame me bitterly for not helping, some are determined not to be helped. Some thank me profusely when we both know they have not got what they came for and neither of us have had the courage to face up to it. Some fix up the old ways and trundle off on their way to the next crisis. Some say they'll call in a week or two and never do. Some stay.

And sometimes something miraculous happens; in response to some barely conscious cue, in the midst of some dark moment or when breaking some awkward silence, I hear my voice drop half an octave, words falling from my lips that strike me as deeply as they appear to strike the person sitting opposite me. We are both captivated by the expression of some simple truth. I know it is not just me that is speaking but that I am speaking on behalf of both of us. I know that without me these words would not be spoken, could not be recognised. They are never fancy, never too far removed from simple common sense, and they contain no answers. If I wrote down some examples they would probably seem commonplace and yet at the time of speaking they are pervaded with poignancy and acceptance. They are spoken from heart to heart and they transform the mundane, the difficult and the perplexing into a golden crown of understanding.

Sometimes in the course of therapy a window opens: the casement is the heart and the voice that reaches through it from another realm speaks not just for you, not just for me, but for *us* and infinitely more than us. It has no truck with the psychological theories that say what should happen and when; it cuts across the conventions of therapy and short-circuits the linearity of thought. I am sure that every experienced therapist recognises it, but what governs the mute hinges of that window? What graceful hand reaches out and unlocks its catch? I have tried and tried to produce the effect, but it is not in my power to do so. I have prayed and pleaded for that gentle breath to envelop us when I felt a client needed it, but to no avail; it has its own reasons, its own timing, its own pace.

On other occasions it has demanded access, like some majestic presence pacing impatiently at the door and then flooding into the room, bringing with it a timeless ocean of stillness and peace. But it will not come unless it is invited. It seems that the only power my client or I have is to prevent it by ignoring it, misinterpreting it or fearing it. Either one of us can deny the soul. In meditation the soul speaks in privacy, but in the context of counselling and therapy it has no interest in the lonely, the isolated or the solitary; it pervades the relationship rather than the individual and where groups are gathered it is even more powerful.

There are a great many things that a therapist does or does not do in order to create the right environment for healing and release, but these things alone cannot produce the actual healing. That, of course, is the province of the soul, the soul activated by the Creator. Not the image of a dry paper soul that has been promulgated by the old Church – that pious, ethereal figure in white robes that will float back to God once we are dead. No, a soul that is utterly of God, that is all of who I am, filled with dark shadows and flickering lights, a soul that is moist, passionate and eternal. A soul that will wait patiently for centuries and will then dash us time and again on the rocks of despair, tear us from our loved ones and destroy our hopes if that is what it takes to get us to recognise its existence; a soul that will do all this, the most terrible work in creation, because of its love for us.

The purpose of the soul is not just to teach but also to learn, to learn in all kinds of ways but mainly to learn from the experience of life. Through this we may develop qualities that can be expressed back into life and thus once again enrich and become one with the Creator – qualities like tolerance, patience, compassion and understanding. Such qualities are not learned from books, nor are they learned from sitting at home. As William Blake says, it is the crooked path that is the path of genius, and we learn as much from trespass as we do from walking the straight and narrow path. So while experience unavoidably takes us through joy and pain it is inevitably the pain, the suffering, that makes people turn to therapists and counsellors for help. Then the wounding must be understood, healed and transformed into wisdom in the crucible of the heart, and the counsellors who help must be versed in the ways of the soul; they must have passed that way themselves.

When the soul is ready, when the timing is right and the preparation is carefully done, soul inspires through the therapist the necessary words to light the flame under that crucible. The hand that touches the tinder is the voice, not the voice of anger or criticism but a voice surrendered to soul. When tone, inflection, cadence and timing are crafted by the energy of love, what a beautiful instrument it becomes: like a bridge of healing that will span the gulf created by any amount of wounding. But before the tinder can be touched that crucible must be charged, charged with the truth that dwells behind the rationalisations, the defences, the avoidance of the wounding that life brings. The soul responds to the honest, to those who are prepared to move a little closer to their deepest, darkest feelings, their despair, their heartache, the suffering of their deepest truth. In that deepest truth the heart cries into the wilderness and the soul responds.

I am not suggesting that suffering be pursued as a required part of developing spiritually, but that our attitude to suffering is a very important part of spiritual development. We create a hundred times more suffering through the avoidance of feeling difficulty and pain than through the feelings themselves. But fortunately the soul is not as hard a taskmaster. As soon as we accept the simple thing that we have been avoiding and acknowledge our need, we are made whole. The soul pours salve onto our wounds in abundance.

The lessons of life cannot be learned by the soul alone, however; neither can they be rendered into understanding by the personality alone. Depth and wisdom are learned from the interaction of soul and self at the instigation of the Creator, but for this to happen we must understand our childhood and what our defences protect. Defences are not just our means of dealing with childhood pain; they are our way of distancing ourselves from accepting the journey of our soul, a soul which has unerringly plotted a course through those experiences for the benefit of our learning. Defences are the way we distance ourselves from the soul's agenda with all its implications: that we are not as free and powerful as we thought we were, that actions have consequences, that we are limited, that life is not only terribly short but is also designed to confront us with having to accept many things that are uncomfortable and disagreeable, and that ultimately we defy the will of the Creator at our mortal peril.

Just as psychological theory suggests that someone outside the self is a necessary part of recapitulating childhood and building ego strength so, I believe, the process I have described is the soul's way of ensuring that its voice is reflected in the therapeutic relationship. It is not just possible for the soul of one person to speak directly to the soul of another: it is desirable, even necessary. That voice cannot be rehearsed or planned; it is always spontaneous, always from beyond the conscious mind and spoken through the heart. It cannot be contrived. It imposes nothing and is instantly recognisable as the voice of true authority. It speaks from the shared understanding and wisdom of both therapist and client and requires only the genuine acknowledgement of need in order to be heard. It is my belief that such moments are activated by the Creator, answering the cries of humanity. It is this voice, often spoken in the first instance through the therapist, that enables people to recognise the truth of their own hearts, because in what is spoken and the way in which it is spoken, they recognise the voice of their own soul.

What then is the role of the therapist? The first thing is to recognise this simple reality: that it is not the counsellor who heals; we and our clients are subject to far greater forces than we may think we are, even those of us who are as sophisticated and clever as we psychotherapists are. We are subject to the movements and the mysteries of the soul, and the soul has its own agenda. The role of the therapist is to stand under that energy, the energy of soul, and help clients understand it and accept it. The role of the therapist is to ask him- or herself what it is that prevents themselves from listening, from hearing the cue and from speaking spontaneously, hardly knowing what will be said, allowing the hand of soul to reach through their heart and touch the heart of another.

Fear is the greatest enemy of soul, fear in service of survival. It is the devil that has plagued me as I have written this essay. I think that those who read it will be better educated than I; they will have heard it all before, they will criticise, ridicule, find my style too adjectival or rhetorical, ignore what I have to say. I fear that I will expose what is most precious in me to what is most barbaric in them. It is ironic that the same voice that can be the means of such healing has in the past been the agent of such terrible destruction that I hardly dare speak of what I care most about. Stick to the rules, stick to the code of ethics, read the books, get it perfect, join a professional organisation, quote from Jung – but whatever you do, don't risk yourself.

Of course my audience is myself; perhaps all that criticism and misunderstanding once came from my parents, my peers, my teachers or society itself, but now it is in me and I see it in you. It is I who shackle my heart in the cold iron of criticism. What a terrible tragedy to be both jailer and jailed! But it is not surprising, especially in this day and age. A thousand years ago people feared the sword, pestilence and famine, but now it is the word that leaves people trembling in fear. We see it every day – a wrong word to the wrong reporter, and a life and career are destroyed overnight.

But I did write, and now you are reading what I have written, and if you have got this far then I imagine you have found at least some of it agreeable. Perhaps the hand that guides you is guiding me too, and there is more that binds us than separates us. The African in her tribe, the white man at his computer, the yellow people at their work and the red folk guarding the land: what we all have in common, before gender, before race, before wealth and health, is a heart. A heart, a soul and – if we allow it – the capacity to feel and to be touched deeply by what we see and experience. And when we touch one another, perhaps it is the hand of God that stirs our hearts. Few are better placed than therapists and counsellors to realise this, to participate in and witness the most wonderful of transformations, the kiss of God gently awakening the souls of slumbering children and whispering, 'You belong to me.'

✡